PRAISE FOR *THE HUSKY EFFECT*

❝Success is about doing your work in a way that it can't be done any better. That is the goal every day, both on the basketball court and at the UConn School of Business.❞

—GENO AURIEMMA,
WINNINGEST BASKETBALL COACH IN NCAA HISTORY,
ELEVEN-TIME NATIONAL CHAMPION

❝Huskies have a championship mentality with a growth mindset, intrinsic motivation to achieve and innovate, and a strong sense of belonging. We build resilience in the students and prepare them for a rewarding life, career, and citizenship.❞

—RADENKA MARIC,
PRESIDENT, UNIVERSITY OF CONNECTICUT

❝Toni Boucher's unwavering commitment to innovation has transformed UConn's School of Business into a powerhouse of entrepreneurial success. *The Husky Effect* takes readers inside the bold initiatives—cutting-edge, hands-on learning in venture investing and groundbreaking research in entrepreneurship—that are equipping the next generation of trailblazers. This is the story of how one donor's vision is building the future, one entrepreneur at a time.❞

—GREG REILLY,
INTERIM DEAN, UCONN SCHOOL OF BUSINESS

❝Toni Boucher's financial and personal commitment to UConn is unparalleled. Her devotion to Connecticut, the university, and our student-athletes has been incredible and has improved the lives of so many. I have known Toni for years, and I am inspired by her selfless devotion to serving and commitment to UConn. She is a state treasure.❞

—MARC D'AMELIO,
COFOUNDER AND CEO, D'AMELIO BRANDS & D'AMELIO FOOTWEAR;
FOUNDER, D'AMELIO HUSKIES NIL COLLECTIVE

❝Toni's generous gift to UConn's now Boucher Management & Entrepreneurship Department has unlocked countless opportunities for students. Thanks to her investment, I've led transaction teams investing real dollars in innovative startups and visited preeminent financial institutions like Apollo Global Management and Fortress Investment Group to underwrite their funds. Her vision for fostering entrepreneurship at UConn will impact generations of Huskies to come.❞

—ARIA PENNA,
FINANCE MAJOR, UCONN CLASS OF 2025

www.amplifypublishinggroup.com

THE HUSKY EFFECT: *How UConn Is Creating the Entrepreneurs of the Future*

©2025 Toni Boucher. All Rights Reserved. No part of this publication may be reproduced, stored in a retrieval system, or transmitted in any form by any means electronic, mechanical, or photocopying, recording, or otherwise without the permission of the author.

Although the author and publisher have made every effort to ensure that the information in this book was correct at press time, the author and publisher do not assume and hereby disclaim any liability to any party for any loss, damage, or disruption caused by errors or omissions, whether such errors or omissions result from negligence, accident, or any other cause.

Author's note: Some company names in the manuscript have been changed for privacy and confidentiality reasons. All the details regarding these companies are accurate. University of Connecticut statistics and demographics cited throughout the book came from publicly available university data.

For more information, please contact:
Amplify Publishing, an imprint of Amplify Publishing Group
620 Herndon Parkway, Suite 220
Herndon, VA 20170
info@amplifypublishing.com

ISBN-13: 979-8-89138-708-9

Printed in the United States

For Guy Iannuzzi and Paul Boucher, who partnered with my husband, Bud, to take him on an unimaginable entrepreneurial adventure.

THE HUSKY EFFECT

HOW UCONN IS CREATING THE ENTREPRENEURS OF THE FUTURE

TONI BOUCHER

WITH JOSH YOUNG

amplify
an imprint of Amplify Publishing Group

CONTENTS

Prologue: **The Spirit of Innovation**	1
1. **Building a University for the Future**	3
2. **A New Vision for Education**	13
3. **An Entrepreneur's Journey**	23
4. **The Education of an Entrepreneur**	35
5. **The Story of The Tile Company**	51
6. **Realizing a Legacy**	59
7. **You Get What You Give**	67
8. **The Entrepreneurship Ecosystem**	73
9. **Investing in Tomorrow**	87
Epilogue: **The UConn Husky Effect**	99
Photo Credits	103
About the Author	105

PROLOGUE: THE SPIRIT OF INNOVATION

THE STATE OF CONNECTICUT has long been known as the birthplace of invention. Since early colonial times, when it served as the marketplace of the original thirteen colonies, Connecticut has been a cradle of American ingenuity and entrepreneurship. This small state has produced a remarkable array of inventions that have changed everyday life: the cotton gin, Colt firearms, *Webster's Dictionary*, the first practical submarine, the Polaroid camera, the Frisbee, and even the lollipop.

Perhaps more importantly, Connecticut has pioneered something less tangible but equally vital: a culture of innovation. It was here that entrepreneurs learned to take risks, to see opportunities where others saw obstacles, and to turn ideas into reality. This spirit of innovation wasn't limited to individual inventors—it created entire industries and transformed the American economy.

Today, the state is channeling that same entrepreneurial spirit in new ways. In an era where technology and innovation are reshaping every aspect of our lives, Connecticut is once again positioning itself at the forefront of change. At the heart of this transformation is the University of Connecticut, the state's flagship public university, which is reimagining how we nurture and develop the entrepreneurs of tomorrow.

This is a story about that transformation—about how a traditional university is adapting to meet the challenges of the future, about the power of experiential learning, and about how one family's journey through the ups and downs of entrepreneurship led to an investment in that future. But more than that, it's a story about the enduring power of innovation and the importance of teaching each new generation not just what to learn but how to think.

BUILDING A UNIVERSITY FOR THE FUTURE

On a crisp spring morning in 2024, the energy was electric in State Farm Stadium in Glendale, Arizona. As Bill Murray's face appeared on the Jumbotron during the NCAA men's basketball championship game, the arena erupted. The actor, whose son Luke serves as an assistant coach for the UConn men's team, rolled up his sleeve and flexed his muscle, sending the crowd into a frenzy. The rhythmic chant that followed—"U ... CONN! U ... CONN! U ... CONN!"—made the temporary risers shake with such force that some fans worried about their stability.

This moment, with a Hollywood star leading cheers for a basketball powerhouse, would have seemed impossible to the founders of the modest Storrs Agricultural School in 1881. Named after brothers Charles and Augustus Storrs, who donated the land and initial funding, the school's mission was practical and focused: educate Connecticut's farmers and laborers in modern agricultural methods.

The transformation from that humble beginning to today's major research university mirrors Connecticut's own evolution from agricultural and industrial power to innovation hub. In 1893, the school became a land-grant college under the Morrill Act of 1862, part of a national movement to create institutions that would teach agriculture, home economics, mechanical arts, and other practical professions. It was a pivotal moment that set the stage for future growth.

The next major transformation came in 1939 when the institution took its current name, and the trustees enacted a plan that divided the university into separate schools and colleges in business, education, home economics, arts, sciences, and agriculture. The School of Social Work and the School of Nursing would soon follow, creating the foundation for a comprehensive university.

The business school, established in 1941, has grown into a major force for innovation and economic development in Connecticut. Today, it operates across four locations—the main campus in Storrs and satellite campuses in Hartford, Stamford, and Waterbury—offering bachelor's, master's, and doctorate degrees. While relatively small compared to the overall university enrollment (with 2,956 undergraduates and more than 1,668 graduate students out of a total student body of over 24,000), the business school has become increasingly central to UConn's mission of driving economic growth and innovation in Connecticut.

The rise of UConn basketball has been more than just a sports story—it has become a catalyst for the university's broader transformation. The women's program, under legendary coach Geno Auriemma since 1985, has achieved unprecedented success: eleven NCAA national championships, including ten since 2000, with six perfect seasons. The men's program, building on Jim

Calhoun's foundation of three national titles between 1999 and 2012, has added two more under Dan Hurley, including back-to-back titles in 2023 and 2024 for a total of six.

This basketball success has created what we call the "UConn Husky Effect." After the men's team won their fifth NCAA Championship in 2023, applications for the 2024 fall semester hit a record high with more than 56,700 applicants, up from 48,000 in 2023 and 43,000 in 2022. This surge in applications has allowed the university to become increasingly selective, raising the academic profile of incoming classes while maintaining its commitment to accessibility and diversity. This improvement in academic profiles of the incoming students has had a significant impact on the school's national rankings.

The basketball program's impact extends far beyond admissions numbers. Both Auriemma and Hurley have created cultures of excellence that influence the entire university. The winningest coach in NCAA history, Auriemma served as the Olympic coach and was the only coach who won gold medals in the 2012 and 2016 Summer Olympics. He is known for his saying: "It is about doing in a way that can't be done any better. That is the goal every day." Every player who has fulfilled all four years of eligibility during his nearly forty-year tenure has earned her degree, demonstrating Auriemma's commitment to academic success.

The coaches' influence extends into the broader community as well. Auriemma hosts the popular Geno Auriemma Leadership Conference, a two-day event that draws senior business executives and academic experts to discuss personal career growth and leadership development. Hurley has shown similar commitment to community engagement, as demonstrated by his support of Aubrien Jimenez, a thirteen-year-old fan battling a rare form of cancer, and his family.

The UConn men's basketball team, led by Coach Dan Hurley, visited Joe Biden at the White House after their 2024 national championship.

The success of the basketball programs has also helped build a powerful alumni network. Two alumni-driven "name, image, and likeness" (NIL) collectives—Bleeding Blue for Good and the D'Amelio Huskies Collective—have been established to support student athletes while encouraging community engagement. These initiatives help attract and retain top talent while instilling values of philanthropy and community service.

But while basketball may have put UConn in the national spotlight, it's the university's academic transformation that is truly revolutionary. Entering 2024, UConn had risen to forty-sixth overall in the *Wall Street Journal* rankings and ninth among public universities. The business school tied with UMass for the top public undergraduate business education in New England, ranking forty-sixth overall in *U.S. News & World Report*'s national rankings. It has also brought prestige to the brand and has helped the university recruit top academics from the US and abroad.

This academic rise reflects a fundamental shift in how UConn approaches education. The university has begun moving beyond the forty-year-old model of traditional academics into real-world interactivity and engagement. The business school, in particular, has embraced experiential learning, understanding that today's rapidly changing economy requires more than just technical knowledge—it demands creativity, adaptability, and entrepreneurial thinking.

This transformation couldn't be more timely. Student demand for entrepreneurship education rose 66 percent during the first two years of the COVID-19 pandemic, reflecting a growing recognition that traditional career paths are evolving. As a land-grant university, UConn has an obligation to ensure its research and education have direct economic impact on the state, and entrepreneurship has become a key vehicle for fulfilling that responsibility.

The university has maintained its commitment to accessibility throughout this transformation. Of those attending UConn in 2024, more than 8,600 were first-generation college students, and over 15,000 students received financial aid totaling some $236 million. This commitment to providing opportunities for all students, regardless of background, remains central to UConn's mission and its vision for the future.

The evolution of UConn's curriculum reflects changing student priorities and workforce demands. Liberal arts and sciences, particularly engineering, continue to be the bedrock of a UConn education, but the university has begun reimagining its Common Curriculum. Five years ago, UConn started revising its core requirements with a new perspective on what modern learning content should look like, moving beyond traditional subject areas to incorporate broader skills and perspectives.

The business school has become particularly active in this transformation. For the first time, it has proposed courses for inclusion in the Common Curriculum, creating a four-course program focused on law, brand management, entrepreneurship, and financial literacy. This represents a significant shift from the traditional view of business education as separate from general education requirements.

The school has also launched new programs responding to changing student priorities. Today's students are increasingly focused on sustainability, social purpose, and finding employers who care about their development and impact. In response, UConn has created a new Master of Science in Social Responsibility in Business degree and developed new courses in modern entrepreneurship that are open to students across the university.

UConn's evolution into a major research university has also positioned it as a crucial engine for Connecticut's economic development. The numbers tell a compelling story: the university contributes $6.9 billion annually to the state's economy.

This local impact has become increasingly important as Connecticut works to maintain its position as an innovation hub. The state faces significant challenges: an aging population, changing industrial base, and competition from other regions for talent and investment. UConn has responded by focusing on developing the workforce pipeline and identifying emerging job opportunities that don't exist yet.

The university has taken a particular interest in supporting small and medium-sized companies, which make up 80 percent of Connecticut's economy. Through partnerships, internships, and research collaborations, UConn helps these businesses access the talent, technology, and resources they need to grow and innovate.

The business school has been particularly active in building bridges between academia and industry. Through its various centers and institutes, it facilitates research partnerships, provides consulting services, and creates opportunities for students to work on real-world projects. These connections help ensure that academic programs remain relevant to industry needs while providing valuable experiences for students.

The Connecticut Center for Entrepreneurship and Innovation (CCEI) has been particularly successful in this regard. Over the past decade, CCEI and its campus partners have helped launch numerous companies while engaging thousands of students, alumni, and community members in entrepreneurial activities. The center has provided more than $2 million to over 1,400 entrepreneurs in many different fields.

The Peter J. Werth Institute for Entrepreneurship and Innovation, established in 2017 with a $22.5 million gift from Peter Werth (later increased to around $30 million), has further strengthened UConn's entrepreneurial ecosystem. The institute serves as a hub connecting resources, programs, academic courses, funding, mentorship, and activities related to entrepreneurship and innovation throughout the university.

"An investment in UConn is an investment in the university's spirit of innovation," Werth said when establishing the institute. "While I didn't attend UConn, I have come to believe in its mission and see the importance of creating opportunities for innovation at our state's flagship university. I'm delighted and honored that I could make this gift in support of young entrepreneurs, as they create innovative solutions for today's unique challenges."

Traditional business education has typically focused on junior and senior years, while freshmen and sophomores were limited to Common Core classes. UConn has shifted this model, allowing students to engage with business school curriculum from day one. Programs like the Business Connections Learning Community provide opportunities for students to expand their business knowledge by networking with fellow students, faculty, and alumni from their first semester on campus.

The university has also recognized the changing nature of career preparation. A new NIL minor has been developed—not just for athletes but for writers, producers, and musicians who want to learn about building their personal brands. The focus is on both the entrepreneurial aspects and the business fundamentals, including understanding legal and financial issues.

This comprehensive approach to education extends beyond traditional business skills. The business school continuously encourages students to be purposeful, intentional, and self-aware. Rather than just studying concepts, students are encouraged to study their own behavior and develop emotional intelligence. These skills are seen as critical for relationship building both in school and later in life.

As UConn looks to the future, it aims to become a top-tier public research university while maintaining its commitment to accessibility and economic impact. The university's leadership recognizes that this requires continued innovation in both what is taught and how it is taught. The success of programs like the **Boucher Management & Entrepreneurship Department** and **Hillside Ventures** shows the potential of this approach.

The transformation of UConn from a regional agricultural school to a national leader in entrepreneurship education mirrors Connecticut's own evolution from colonial marketplace to modern innovation hub. It's a story of vision, persistence, and adaptation—the very qualities that define successful entrepreneurs. As the university continues to evolve, it remains focused on its core mission: preparing students to solve the challenges of tomorrow while driving economic growth and innovation in Connecticut.

A NEW VISION FOR EDUCATION

THE FIRST TIME I MET RADENKA MARIC, I was struck by how different she was from the typical university president. Here was a distinguished chemical engineer who was also an accomplished painter and pianist, an amateur chef who spoke four languages fluently (Croatian, English, German, and Japanese), and someone who designed and made much of her own wardrobe. But what truly set her apart wasn't just this remarkable combination of talents—it was her revolutionary vision for transforming higher education.

To understand that vision, you need to understand Radenka's journey. Growing up in working-class Yugoslavia, she learned early on about the power of education to transform lives. At sixteen, she won the Yugoslavian national championship in science, marking her as someone special. She graduated from the University of Belgrade in 1989 and began what seemed like a promising career at the Serbian Academy of Science and Art.

Then history intervened. Yugoslavia began its violent dissolution in 1991 after the collapse of the Soviet Union, with republics splitting off amid ethnic tensions and economic collapse. As her homeland descended into civil war, Radenka made a decision that would shape her future approach to education and life: she chose to pursue graduate studies in Japan.

UConn President Radenka Maric

"I was never afraid to be first, to open the door, and to stand at the door to let others in," she reflects. This wasn't just bravado. She became the first woman to receive a PhD from Kyoto University's school of engineering in 1996, a remarkable achievement in Japan's traditionally male-dominated academic environment.

Her next step was equally bold. She joined Toyota Motor Corporation as their first woman engineer, where she was often mistaken for a secretary. But rather than stay in this prestigious position, she took another risk. When recruited by nGimat, a startup in Atlanta with just two employees, she left her secure job at Toyota—complete with a paid apartment, car, and generous benefits—to pursue a new challenge.

"When I left Toyota, my boss said to me, 'How can you leave this? You have a paid apartment, a paid car, paid travel, and a performance bonus,'" she recalls. "Yes, it's very difficult when you are being given those things to say, 'No, I'm leaving and taking this risk because I'm ready to take the risk.' It might have been completely unknown and in a different country, but I did it because I wanted to challenge myself."

At nGimat, which produced nanopowders used in everything

from scratchproof eyeglasses to anti-graffiti coatings, Radenka learned firsthand about entrepreneurship. As one of only three employees, she did everything from marketing to production to sales to cleaning the office. This experience would profoundly influence her approach to education and leadership.

"Your growth in any startup depends on your ability to do everything, and there can't be any excuses, or it won't work," she explains. "When you have limited resources, you have to think differently."

One particular experience at nGimat exemplified this principle. She was tasked with making a copying powder product that typically required a $100,000 investment in equipment. The company had only $100 to spend. Rather than declare the task impossible, she went to the machine shop herself and figured out how to produce one pound of the powder. This proof of concept allowed her to show potential clients how the process could be scaled up with more investment.

"If I had stayed with Toyota, I would've said, 'Okay, we will just use the latest technology and buy the highest value products we need,'" she explains. "But if you are at a startup where you don't have the resources and you don't have the people and you can invest only $100 in a project, that's when you start thinking differently. So that's what I tell people: you have to experience both."

After leaving nGimat, Radenka moved to Canada to serve as **Director of Science and Technology at the National Research Council (NRC)**, Canada's largest research organization. There, she worked on groundbreaking projects, including a hydrogen highway stretching from Whistler, British Columbia, to San Diego, California. In 2015, she became Chief Technology Officer at Health eSense, developing a handheld, noninvasive device for monitoring chronic illnesses through breath analysis.

But at age forty-four, Radenka made another unexpected pivot: she entered academia. "As an entrepreneur, you always have to challenge yourself and put yourself into the unknown where it's uncomfortable," she says. "It's like walking with a little rock in your shoe. You still can walk, but it hurts a little bit. It can also hurt you financially because you don't know the outcome."

Her goal wasn't just to teach—it was to influence younger generations. She joined UConn in 2010 as chair professor in the **Department of Chemical Biomolecular Engineering** and the **Materials Science and Engineering** program, two of the university's most prestigious departments. She also led the ambitious Eminent Faculty Initiative in Sustainable Energy, a partnership between UConn, the Connecticut General Assembly, and industrial partners, aimed at putting Connecticut on the international stage in sustainable energy development.

Her impact was immediately apparent. In 2015, she became executive director of the UConn Technology Park Innovation Partnership Building (IPB), overseeing a state-of-the-art $200 million facility focused on advanced manufacturing, cybersecurity, system engineering, and advanced characterization laboratories. Two years later, she was named vice president for research, innovation, and entrepreneurship, managing a $300 million research budget across UConn's twelve colleges and schools.

When she was appointed interim president of UConn in February 2022, and then named the seventeenth president that September, she brought a radically different perspective to the role. "People ask me, 'Did you ever dream of being president of UConn?'"she says. "I say absolutely not, because I didn't plan to do any of the things I have done. Most university presidents come from a liberal arts background, while I am an engineer. But no matter your background, my feeling is that you have to be a visionary, you have to be aspirational, and you have to move people with you."

Her vision for UConn is built on five pillars: creativity, innovation, entrepreneurship, financial literacy, and emotional intelligence. This last element might seem surprising coming from an engineer, but Radenka sees it as crucial for student success.

"Emotional intelligence is so important for self-awareness, for resilience, for courage, for persistence, and if we don't teach that to our students, they're lost," she explains. "Mental health problems have been increasing and increasing and increasing at universities because of lack of self-awareness, lack of knowing who you are, and lack of believing that you can succeed."

This holistic approach extends to financial literacy, an area traditionally overlooked in university education. When a retired Wall Street executive started a no-credit financial literacy club meeting for three hours on Friday afternoons in 2023, skeptics doubted anyone would attend. Instead, the class was overbooked, attracting students from across disciplines, particularly women majoring in nursing, arts, and science-related fields.

The business school has also developed a financial literacy program for high school students, bringing seniors to campus on Saturdays to work with college students. They cover basics like different types of bank accounts, how loans work, and the best strategies for paying for college. The goal isn't to recruit students to UConn but to provide crucial life skills often missing from traditional education.

Radenka's approach to understanding student needs is equally revolutionary. "How do you do customer discovery if you never ask the customers? Who are our customers? Our customers are our students," she says. Direct conversations with students revealed their top five priorities: academic success, mental health, financial literacy, entrepreneurial opportunities, and climate change. This insight has helped align faculty priorities and resource allocation.

"My tagline from day one when I became president is student first, UConn always," Radenka explains. "People ask, 'What do you mean by student first?' I tell them that everything we do, every priority we identify, we are going to ask ourselves, 'How is this going to help our students' success?' And if it's not helping our students' success, then we need to ask why we are doing it."

Radenka's vision for UConn reflects her understanding of how today's students differ from previous generations. Research shows that they overwhelmingly prefer to work for purpose-driven companies rather than focusing solely on financial gain. This preference extends even to the financial sector, where many young people insist on green technology and climate-saving investments as their focus.

"What gives me hope is that young people are very purpose oriented," she says. "They don't want the car; they want smaller apartments that leave smaller carbon footprints. The older generation's validation was 'How big is your house? How many cars do you have?' The young people today cannot care less about any of those. Their awareness to purpose is why we need to empower more young people to lead."

This shift in priorities has profound implications for how UConn approaches education. The university has begun emphasizing off-campus work, whether through internships or community volunteer work, to help students understand real-world needs and become agents of change.

"Many times, innovation happens out of necessity," Radenka explains. "It's about observing the real world and all of its challenges. It's about putting yourself in different settings, experiencing them, and then letting your brain speak. If you are never exposed to these challenges, then it's very hard to think differently."

The results of this new approach are already evident. Over the past decade, UConn's physical plant has been visibly upgraded with a new library, material sciences building, business school building, hockey arena, and recreational center. But the more significant changes are happening behind the scenes, in how students learn and develop.

By 2024, as mentioned in the previous chapter, UConn had risen to forty-sixth overall in the *Wall Street Journal* rankings and ninth among public universities. The university is also number one among public universities in time to degree, averaging 4.1 years, with an 85 percent graduation rate. Radenka is pushing to raise that above 90 percent, often saying, "The most expensive education and degree is one that you don't have."

However, implementing this vision comes with significant challenges, particularly in funding. As a public university, only 19 percent of UConn's funding comes from the state, just over $400 million of a $2 billion-plus budget. Maintaining and increasing this funding requires convincing 187 state legislators, each with different priorities, that investing in UConn is investing in Connecticut's future.

Radenka approaches this challenge thoughtfully. "When I think of education, I have to think of the Connecticut economy," she says. "I call it a dialogue. I don't call it a challenge. I call it a moment for me to pause and listen. What are the concerns? How can I help the communities?"

She makes a compelling case by comparing UConn's impact to that of other institutions. While Yale enrolls only 5 percent of Connecticut residents (with 15 percent staying after graduation),

72 percent of UConn students are from Connecticut, and 77 percent remain in the state. The university's economic impact is substantial: $6.9 billion annually flows back into the state's economy because of UConn.

Radenka could easily close UConn's budget gap by accepting more international students who pay full tuition. In 2022, there were 6,000 qualified international students who applied. However, since only 2 percent typically remain in Connecticut after graduation, this would not serve the state's long-term interests.

"I'm purposely losing money by taking Connecticut students and subsidizing their scholarships," she explains, noting that about 15,000 students receive some $250 million annually in financial aid. "But if I don't do that, there will be no future workforce for the Connecticut economy."

Her focus is particularly on small to medium-sized companies, which comprise 80 percent of Connecticut's economy. UConn is asking big questions like "How does the state increase its workforce pipeline?" and "How does it identify jobs that can be created that don't currently exist?"

The university is also expanding its role in entrepreneurship education. The Connecticut Center for Entrepreneurship and Innovation (CCEI) has provided more than $2 million to over 1,400 entrepreneurs in many different fields. Success stories range from ProVelocity Bat, a baseball training tool, to Bastion, the first specialty digital clinic focused on men's reproductive and prostate health.

For Radenka, leadership is about continually pushing boundaries. "Instead of saying I can't do this or that, go with your passion, go with your vision, do the new things, challenge yourself," she says. "When people ask me, 'What is next?' I say, 'I never know what is next.' But I always ask myself, 'Is what I'm doing challenging me? Is this something that I believe brings value to society?' And if I say yes, then I am in the right place."

This philosophy has helped transform UConn from a traditional state university into an innovative institution preparing students for the challenges of tomorrow. But to understand how this vision is being implemented in practice, we need to look at the story of one entrepreneur whose journey would ultimately help make many of these changes possible.

3 AN ENTREPRENEUR'S JOURNEY

Winston Churchill once said, "Success is moving from failure to failure without a loss of enthusiasm." If anyone embodied this spirit, it was my late husband, Henry "Bud" Boucher. Through multiple ventures, countless setbacks, and persistent innovation, his entrepreneurial journey exemplified both the promise and perils of building businesses without formal training or support systems. His story illustrates why proper entrepreneurial education is so crucial for future generations.

Entrepreneurs are defined by more than just their business acumen. They possess a high level of intelligence, confidence, creativity, a dedicated work ethic, a very deep, personal level of ambition—and a great deal of stamina. Freedom and passion are their main motivators, not making money or becoming rich. Money is usually the byproduct or the result of their efforts. Bud personified these traits, though his path to entrepreneurship was anything but direct.

Bud's first dream was to become a pilot. In his senior year of high school, he received provisional acceptance into the United States Air Force Academy, but at the last minute, the son of a major donor to their US Senator took his spot. Bud was crushed and had to scramble to find a college with an Air Force ROTC program. He discovered **Saint Michael's College** in Vermont, an all-male school at the time, with the bonus of a nationally recognized unarmed drill team.

Rather than let the disappointment define him, Bud threw himself into the ROTC program at Saint Michael's. His natural leadership abilities emerged as he became captain of the drill team, leading them to two national championships. This early experience of turning setback into success would become a pattern throughout his life.

After graduating, he joined the Air Force and was stationed at Sheppard Air Force Base in Texas. He seemed to have his career path set as a fighter jet pilot, traveling to other bases for training. Shortly after we married, he was stationed at Ellsworth Air Force Base, a few miles outside of Rapid City, South Dakota, an area best known for nearby Mount Rushmore and minus-fifty-degree weather in the winter.

But as the Vietnam War wound down, the Air Force reduced its need for pilots and pulled back its investment in pilot training. If Bud couldn't be a pilot, he didn't want to stay in the military. Before being discharged, he decided to pursue a graduate degree in economics and accounting at **South Dakota State University** with tuition paid for by the Armed Services. Though he didn't want to be a CPA or auditor, he saw this as a stepping stone to the burgeoning field of management consulting.

Bud's entry into the business world came at **Waddell & Reed**, an asset and financial planning firm based in Kansas City. He had a natural affinity for economics and was an accomplished mathematician, making him well-suited for financial analysis. But even in this early stage of his career, his entrepreneurial mindset was evident. Rather than focusing solely on his assigned tasks, he was constantly looking for ways to improve processes and identify new opportunities.

His boss at Waddell & Reed, Bob Rogers, recognized this innovative spirit and became an important mentor. Rogers would later become a major player at Marion Laboratories and chairman of the Kauffman Foundation (one of the first billion-dollar nonprofits in the US). When Waddell & Reed underwent a major downsizing, Rogers suggested he apply to Touche Ross, one of the biggest CPA firms in the city. That is where he met Ed Kangas, who would later become chairman of Deloitte and Touche.

Bud Boucher in his US Air Force uniform

At **Touche Ross**, Bud's quick mind and exceptional ability to master new subjects served him well. He was hired into the management consulting division, where he could work across multiple industries and learn different business models. His versatility soon became apparent. He became an expert in energy pricing and was asked to testify before Congress during the oil shortages of the 1970s. He consulted on the building of an oil refinery in Belgium, spending two years traveling back and forth across the Atlantic. He was then tasked with developing an asbestos claims facility in the New York area for insurance companies required to cover affected individuals.

But Bud was wired differently from most consultants. Even as he rose to the top of his field, he would grow bored with doing just one thing at a time, even if he was doing it well. He had a photographic memory and an ability to process information and concepts so fast that he was liable to forget a solution to one problem before moving on to the next. This trait, which could be both a blessing and a curse, drove him to constantly seek new challenges and opportunities.

This restless energy wasn't inherited. Bud's dad wasn't like him at all in this regard. Though his dad didn't go to college, he earned a good living working at a tool-and-die business and supplemented his income tending bar on weekends. His mother, who also didn't go to college, went through nursing school and became an RN. When the owner of the tool-and-die business retired and offered Bud's dad the chance to buy the business, he passed. He didn't want the risk. This risk-averse mindset was exactly what Bud would spend his life pushing against.

Even in his younger days, Bud Boucher always had an entrepreneurial spirit.

During our time in Kansas City, Bud's entrepreneurial spirit truly came alive. He became a house flipper long before that became in vogue. He was always planning to build a new house and plotting how to sell the one we were in, figuring out how to take out the profit and use it to build a nicer one. He believed that the equity we accumulated from this would become our retirement fund, as we had virtually no savings.

We ended up building two additional homes simultaneously, one for $45,000 and one for $86,000, and then moving into the one that didn't sell first. Luckily, that was the nicer home, which we would end up selling for $130,000—big money in that day and age. This success gave Bud the confidence to think bigger, but it also perhaps made him overconfident about his ability to spot opportunities.

Because we did so well in Kansas City with the house flipping, Bud decided to expand his reach in real estate. He began combing *The Wall Street Journal* and other publications for opportunities. Soon enough, he found what he thought could be the deal of a lifetime in Florida.

This was a highly speculative venture. The deal called for each investor to put in $1,200 for a part in a huge property on the outskirts of Orlando, betting that a future developer would one day buy up the land for some then-unknown project. Bud did extensive research on Orlando and believed that it was a city poised for growth. We traveled there and took a helicopter ride to look at the property. To me, it looked like a massive swamp, but Bud felt in his gut something big would happen there. In the end, we simply didn't have enough money to make the investment.

Well, Bud had been right. The project ultimately became Disney World! This near miss would haunt him for years, reinforcing his belief that his instincts were good but that lack of capital was holding him back from success.

I didn't see things Bud's way. To me, we were constantly putting what little extra money we had at risk. I felt that this was unnecessary because in my mind, we were already living the American dream. What more could we possibly need or want—especially if we risked losing what we had?

This thinking came from my upbringing. I was born in a tiny bedroom of a farmhouse in rural Italy. While the adults tended the fields during the day, my brother Guy and I were supervised by a black-and-white Border Collie as we played. My father had only a grammar school education, and my mother had none. During World War II while my father, who had been on the front lines in Libya, was a prisoner of war in England, the Nazis destroyed our village.

When I was five and Guy was seven, my parents sold all their possessions to buy steerage-class tickets on a ship bound for America, in search of a better life for their children. The first five years in America were awful. We spoke no English, wore hand-me-down clothes to school, and were discriminated against as poor, uneducated immigrants. My father worked multiple jobs to support us, 24/7.

Growing up the way I did, always on the edge of not knowing where our next meal would come from, made me very, very risk averse. I felt that every dollar we saved for the future should be saved for the future, not invested in some harebrained scheme. This tension between security and risk-taking would define our marriage. However, even when I thought his ideas were crazy and told him so, deep down I secretly believed in him and wanted to support him.

After the successful sojourn in house flipping, Bud began looking to develop things that people needed but didn't have. His first invention was a hands-free **foot washer**. He reasoned that as people grew older or were disabled, they would have a hard time in the shower bending down to wash their feet.

His concept was ingenious in its simplicity: a swivel pump for soap in the middle, with nylon bristle pads on each side. The fact that the soap came out of a pump was itself new, as we had only bar soap at the time. The bather would place their foot on the pump, soap would come out onto the brush, and then they could scrub their feet on the brush. When they were finished, they would rinse each foot under the shower. The apparatus had suction cups on the bottom so it would stay in place and make it unmoveable.

Bud sketched the foot-washer design on a notepad and then made a computer model. He had a prototype manufactured, and it worked perfectly! In June of 1981, he had a notary public confirm his drawing. He planned to file for a patent on the design and then figure out how to raise money to have it manufactured and distributed. But as was often the way with him, he moved on to other things before bringing it to market. He put the foot washer on the shelf for so long that larger companies began making and marketing similar products.

Next was another idea: the **inflatable mattress**. When we were living in Kansas City and I was hired as an executive trainee at the soon-to-be-constructed one-thousand-room Westin Hotel, I befriended a German woman whose son was involved with a new idea for an inflatable mattress called Inflatabed. The concept was to have a mattress you could store in your closet and then inflate when somebody comes to visit, or that you could take on camping trips. The company enlisted Bud as a consultant and developed a prototype.

Bud assembled a few partners to invest. But after the prototype was made, they couldn't agree on how much to invest in the next step, and the whole thing fizzled out. They were like a rock band who couldn't agree on what songs to put on the album. My brother would later point out that one of Bud's weaknesses as an entrepreneur was that he never found appropriate and solid financial backers.

Today, however, the inflate-a-bed concept is a common household item used by millions, but made by other companies.

While we were living in Kansas City, Bud was offered several opportunities to come aboard companies that were consulting clients of his at Touche Ross and bring in his ideas to help them grow. One of those was the offer to become CEO of **Vogel Popcorn**. Fred Vogel, the founder, invited Bud and me to see his operation in Iowa. He had a huge business that supplied popcorn to movie theater chains throughout the country, and he lived in a mansion with a basement stocked with pinball machines and video games. When he showed us into his office, he offered us some popcorn from his movie theater lobby popcorn machine. He turned to Bud and said, "All this could be yours."

As much as I liked Mr. Vogel and his business, I told Bud that I could never live in the middle of Iowa, hundreds of miles from anything. Bud agreed with me and turned down the offer. Looking back, this decision illustrated another challenge entrepreneurs face: balancing business opportunities with family considerations.

Like most entrepreneurs, my husband was always thinking out of the box. He had a folder full of information on companies that he wanted to merge. But sometimes I felt that he wasn't just thinking outside of the proverbial box—he was living outside of the box! Though I didn't realize it at the time, Bud was not only coming up with ideas; he was also testing financial maneuvers that would become common in the high-finance world, like having one company take over a completely unrelated company in what would later be called a reverse merger.

One constant was that Bud was willing to try things far outside his wheelhouse. In the late 1970s, he was approached by a man living in Laurel Canyon in Los Angeles. The man wanted to start an online company selling tapes, videos, and books of the top musicians of the 1960s and 1970s, including Cass Elliot, Joni Mitchell, Carole King, and Frank Zappa. Though Bud knew nothing about the music business, he was asked to help because of his consulting background and business acumen. He immediately said yes because he was a music buff who closely followed those musicians.

The company flew Bud to Los Angeles, and he embedded himself there to sort out how they could market their material and what rights they would need, as most of the music was already being sold in stores. He ended up having a wonderful time and even attended the Grammy Awards, but par for the course, things did not work out as envisioned.

His most significant early venture came when he and one of his colleagues from Touche Ross decided to create **MB Systems**. Based in Norwalk, it serviced old mainframe computers that were being phased out. These mainframes ran McCormack & Dodge software, once the preeminent operating system in business, but one that was becoming overshadowed by faster, more agile software. It was the pure embodiment of Moore's Law, which states that the number of transistors on a computer chip double every twenty-four months, thus making computers smaller and faster. And this obviously impacted their software.

Everybody shook their head at Bud's idea, calling it dated, but he saw a need in the market for these services because companies that still ran McCormack & Dodge had to keep their systems functioning. Most importantly, like other companies he would start, he had plans to expand its services and grow it into something larger. He recruited several professionals, and I helped with the back-office work.

Bud was ahead of his time in many ways, including culturally. One of the men he hired was Black, which wasn't a big deal in Connecticut. But MB Systems had a large school system in Atlanta as a client. Bud wanted to send his Black employee, whom he regarded very highly, to work on their system. I told him it was a bad idea sending a Black man to the Deep South at that time.

"What do you mean?" he asked.

"Many people still harbor prejudices," I said. "He's a Black man. You may lose your biggest client."

"Are you kidding me?" he said, in all seriousness. "He's the best man for the job, so he's going."

Bud was not good at understanding the politics of a situation, which was my strength. He sent him down there, and the man did a great job fixing all the bugs in the system. And, as I had predicted, the client fired MB Systems a week later. Bud's reaction was that if they didn't want his best man working on their system, then he didn't need them as a client. He would stand on principle even if it hurt him financially.

Unfortunately, Bud was not able to transition MB Systems' software maintenance system fast enough before it became obsolete, and MB Systems eventually faded into the woodwork. This pattern of being slightly ahead or behind the curve would repeat itself. It happened again with something called tinplate, an opportunity that arrived by chance, out of left field.

A neighbor of ours in Wilton owned a company called **Tinplate Partners**. It manufactured and sold tinplate, sheets of steel that are coated with a rust-proof layer of tin. This was an older company that had some business, but with decreasing long-term prospects.

Bud got on this slowly sinking ship as an investor and board member. But as tinplate began dying due to other steel products taking its place, Bud desperately came up with a pie-in-the-sky idea to maintain Tinplate Partners as a going concern.

He proposed that the company buy Tropicana, the orange juice company, because our neighbor had a relationship with Seagram's, which owned the company. While Bud had several discussions with Seagram's, the primary obstacle again was capital and discomfort with his nonconventional ideas.

These experiences were teaching Bud valuable lessons about entrepreneurship, though he didn't always apply them immediately. He was learning that having a good idea wasn't enough. You needed the right partners, sufficient capital, perfect timing, and skill in implementing out-of-the-box strategies. But his enthusiasm for new ventures never dimmed. If anything, each setback seemed to fuel his determination to find the next opportunity.

4 THE EDUCATION OF AN ENTREPRENEUR

Though I didn't fully connect the dots when Bud was working on all of his crazy ideas, I began to realize that I had grown up with an entrepreneur: my older brother. Throughout our childhood, Guy was off-the-charts smart. He pulled straight A's without even cracking a book. In art, he could reproduce everything he saw on paper without taking any classes. He could pick up an instrument and play it. He could read a two-hundred-page book in just a few hours. I later learned that he was once given an IQ test, and the result was genius.

My brother's acumen was first noticed when he read over a hundred books in one summer to win a city-wide reading contest after just starting grammar school. He built his first telescope in our garage at age twelve with spare parts he found and bought. In high school, he began to excel in everything—science, literature, history, art, music, you name it. He played the violin in the school string quartet and ended up in the Connecticut all-state orchestra. He painted the rise and fall of the Roman Empire across the auditorium and got an A in Latin (he needed it to keep from failing the class). It galled me because I had to stay up studying until 2 a.m. just to get a B.

My father was fully supportive of Guy's childhood entrepreneurial adventures, and he basked in the praise of his son's accomplishments by the factory executives whose offices he cleaned every night. When Guy told him he needed to buy a $200 laser for his science project for the state fair, my dad gave him the money. But because that was a week's salary, the pressure was on. Guy had better win the Connecticut State Science Fair or else, which of course, he did.

My older brother, Guy

He became president of **Junior Achievement of Connecticut**, a delegate to the National Junior Achievement Conference held at Indiana University, and also became a National Merit Scholarship Semifinalist. When he won the Westinghouse Science scholarship (which now is the Intel scholarship) during his senior year in high school, he was accepted by **Yale University** to enroll as an undergraduate. But there was no way my father could afford the balance of the tuition, so Guy was forced to look elsewhere.

For his part, Guy was desperate to move far from home. He ended up being offered one of only five annual full general scholarships to the **University of Arizona**, which had one of the best astronomy and physics departments in the country with some of the nation's best telescopes.

But on day one at the University of Arizona, the dean of the astronomy/physics department issued a grim warning at the first department student meeting. He told the group, "There are about a hundred of you here. After you graduate four years hence, you all intend to attend our famous graduate school. I have some bad news for you 'superstars.' Maybe two of you will make it—the rest of you will never work in astronomy."

These words were prophetic. In the next two years, almost the entire class ended up struggling and either failing or switching majors. For once, Guy was no exception. Math had always been his weak suit, and he was nothing if not realistic. He saw the writing on the wall and switched his major to psychology, thereby dodging years of frustration.

Unfortunately, when he switched majors, Guy lost his critical scholarship and had to pay his own way. Fortunately, his unusual combination of skills and ability to mix art and science came to the rescue. Leveraging his business savvy and talent led him to acquire freelance advertising work for a variety of department stores in Tucson. Within a few months, he was making more money working ten hours a week than his professors.

Guy also had another unusual experience. His studies in the **Clinical Psychology** program at the university attracted the attention of his professors, who all wanted him to pursue a career in psychology. To help motivate him, they got him an evening job in the psychiatric ward at the county hospital. After two years of work in that hellhole, he swore to never work in psychology again. But the hands-on experience would prove useful.

In his spare time, he took graduate courses in herpetology, ichthyology, and art and collected reptiles from the desert for the Arizona-Sonora Desert Museum. Looking back, I can see that he had a unique combination of brains, curiosity, and psychological insight into extreme personalities. This eclectic mix would serve him well.

It was clear to him that he was going to make far more money working in advertising and design than in the sciences. When he graduated, he went to work full-time in advertising. He got a job at a small advertising agency in Tucson and did well. He then moved to San Diego in 1972 (though Barbara , his first wife, refused to move, thus ending their marriage), where he landed a job as an art director at the second-largest agency in the city, Teawell Advertising. The advertising powerhouse Young & Rubicam later acquired Teawell.

Because of his science background, he gravitated toward aerospace accounts. But after a year in San Diego, disappointed over his small salary raises, he realized that the real money and more opportunities were in Los Angeles, so he moved. There he ended up working for a wide range of ad agencies and large corporations, including **Hughes Aircraft Company, Getty Oil Company, Northrop Grumman,** and **Lockheed Martin.**

He spent a few years In Tehran, Iran, as a marketing director for a company creating a university (and acquired another wife). This experience taught him how to run a marketing department and agency. He put this to good use when he returned to Los Angeles, where he ran the in-house ad agency for **Revell**, one of the largest model toy companies in the country.

Though the money was good and the work rewarding, Guy found the massive traffic and lifestyle issues in LA unbearable, commuting over four hours every day. He missed San Diego. After our parents retired and moved to live with him, he moved back to San Diego with them in 1980.

San Diego was seen as one of the national hubs of aerospace, headquarters for **General Dynamics, Aerojet General**, and other large companies. But instead of taking a job at an ad agency, Guy formed one called **Mentus**. He believed that having his own shop would give him flexibility and allow him to diversify.

All the major San Diego aerospace and technology companies quickly became clients, and he quickly grew Mentus. Not only did he position himself on the ground floor of a large industry, but he was also about to receive an education from some of the most successful entrepreneurs in the country.

"It was all due to the sheer luck of being in the right place at the right time," he says.

To which I would add, "with the right skill set."

I moved to San Diego briefly to help him ramp up Mentus, providing some back-office support. I know I had an impact, not in terms of expertise but in terms of changing how he presented himself. Guy had a real California look, normally wearing baggy jeans and T-shirts, looking like he had just stumbled into the office from a walk on the beach.

Taking a cue from the adage "You never get a second chance to make a good first impression," I went to his apartment, gathered all his old clothes, and donated them to Goodwill. I then went to Nordstrom and bought him an entirely new wardrobe, from suits to shirts to shoes and socks.

At first, not surprisingly, he was not happy. But one day, after he started wearing his new look, he said to me, "Every time I walk in the door, I'm being treated with such respect, and they know nothing about me."

I smiled. "Clothes are how you first present your brand," I replied. "And as you now see, they make a difference."

Guy's contract with Aerojet General, one of his first, turned out to be both lucrative and a learning experience. While working on one of Aerojet's Wall Street presentations, he came across an unknown company called **Hybritech**, a startup with offices in a large trailer a few blocks away. It was founded in 1978 by Ivor Royston and Howard Birndorf, professors at UC San Diego. Within a month, the company received a $300,000 investment from **Kleiner Perkins Caufield & Byers** (now Kleiner Perkins), the iconic venture capital firm based in Silicon Valley.

Hybritech was San Diego's first major biotechnology company, focused on exploring the use of monoclonal antibodies for diagnostics and therapeutics. Their goal was to implement this new science to create better products for research and ultimately therapy. Over time, Hybritech's breakthroughs would include the first blood test to screen for prostate cancer—PSA—and early research into cancer treatments.

Like any good entrepreneur, Guy decided to expand his knowledge. "I was kinda trained as a rocket scientist and astrophysicist, and I knew how to market aerospace and the hard sciences," he explains. "I had never heard of monoclonal antibodies, but I knew enough to know that biotech had potential, and I could get in on the ground floor. How difficult could it be?"

The first thing he noticed was the company's culture. Aside from having offices in a trailer, the place was full of twenty-somethings.

"They were the first real entrepreneurs that I had ever met in my life," Guy says. "They were all around my age, which was really weird because I wasn't used to guys my age running a technology company."

It was also eye-opening to see the effect that a venture capital firm like Kleiner Perkins could have, as VCs were only beginning to be used during that period. Today, of course, venture capital is a multibillion-dollar business that is jump-starting some of the most successful companies.

"I learned that while angel investors and a network of twenty friends putting money into an idea was helpful, if you really wanted to grow and needed real money, your best bet was to find a VC," Guy says. "That was all very new. I learned from the masters about how to make presentations for both investors and VCs."

Hybritech's goal was to raise $10 million through an IPO, so they engaged Mentus to prepare the presentations for Wall Street bankers. As they were moving toward that goal, they had to be very entrepreneurial and find ways to make money. They discovered that antibodies could make good diagnostic products, among other uses. They began making a wide range of diagnostic products and turned to Mentus to create their marketing materials, partly because they liked Guy's science acumen and partly because they could not afford a large ad firm.

The entire Hybritech group, led by its CEO, Ted Greene, took Guy under their wing and put him on a rapid learning curve. With his natural ability to absorb complicated information, he became proficient in the many facets of biotechnology. Mentus ended up creating all its marketing, including its new product launches.

Those included the first diagnostic assays (tests to determine the presence of biological compounds)—which are used to analyze biological markers for an initial diagnosis and then to monitor risk factors—and later, the **prostate-specific antigen (PSA)** test used to detect prostate cancer in men.

"I learned everything about entrepreneurship in emerging companies and technology companies from Hybritech and the many companies that came out of Hybritech," he says. "They had an amazing culture. You could walk into the chairman's office and talk about what was going on and whatever was on your mind (if it was relevant, of course). You could have this kind of open door, this kind of energy, and this kind of spirit. Little did I know, that's not very common (at least within my larger aerospace clients), but it was magical because I experienced the entrepreneurial mindset firsthand."

Guy noticed that these companies functioned in an open forum rather than having a structural hierarchy. This allowed for the spreading of corporate culture and knowledge. Everybody learned quickly. There were twelve vice presidents at Hybritech, and every single one of them went on to create multiple companies—some over a dozen each. Hybritech became a breeding ground for serial entrepreneurs.

Hybritech's technology, along with its modest but growing profits, soon attracted the attention of larger pharmaceutical companies. In 1986, Eli Lilly, seeking a foothold in the monoclonal antibody-based drug and diagnostics business, paid over $450 million in cash and warrants to buy Hybritech, at that point the largest merger and acquisitions (M&A) deal in San Diego.

The company's early success and the wealth it created among its founders and employees spurred other academic scientists to form companies and ultimately led to San Diego becoming a major hub for biotech. After Hybritech, cofounder Birndorf went on to help found a string of biotech companies, including Neurocrine Biosciences, Ligand Pharmaceuticals, Gen-Probe, and IDEC Pharmaceuticals. Gen-Probe was sold to Hologic for $3.7 billion, and IDEC merged with Biogen in a $6.8 billion deal. *The New York Times* dubbed Birndorf "the Johnny Appleseed of the Biotechnology forest."

Today, over a hundred major life science companies in San Diego can trace their lineage to Hybritech, which shows that the entrepreneurial spirit of a few can change the lives of many. In short, the genesis of the biotechnology cluster in San Diego really did come from that company. Now there are nearly twenty-five hundred biotech companies in the country.

Maybe there was something in the San Diego water that sparked entrepreneurship in the late 1970s, because biotech wasn't the only industry of startups that would go on to change the business landscape. By sheer luck for Guy, Hybritech was next door to M/A-COM Linkabit, a company owned by two propeller heads named Irwin Jacobs and Andrew Viterbi, a partnership which down the road would lead to the genesis of **Qualcomm**. Guy struck up a relationship with M/A-COM Linkabit, and in 1981, Mentus went to work for them as their marketing agency, as Guy understood the science and was able to apply the creative marketing skills they needed.

Underpinning their unique skill sets, Jacobs and Viterbi were a different brand of entrepreneurs than we typically think of today. Both had backgrounds rooted in academia. Jacobs started his career as an associate professor of electrical engineering at MIT and then became a professor of computer science and engineering at UC San Diego.

Viterbi, in a coincidental parallel to Guy's life and mine, grew up in Italy and emigrated to the US with his family two years prior to World War II. He earned a BS and an MS from MIT. Then, while working at Raytheon, he earned one of the first doctorates in electrical engineering ever granted at USC. He became a professor of electrical engineering at UCLA and created what is known as the Viterbi algorithm, a mathematical formula to eliminate signal interference—an algorithm that paved the way for the widespread use of cellular technology.

Once Jacobs and Viterbi entered the business world, they were not fly-by-the-seat-of-their-pants entrepreneurs. Owing to their academic backgrounds, they were prepared and studied their surroundings. After growing Linkabit, they merged it with

M/A-COM to create M/A-COM Linkabit. That company was then sold for quite a bit of money, and they and several other partners started Qualcomm to expand their reach. Qualcomm became a pioneer in mobile satellite communication systems. It developed cutting-edge semiconductors and software for wireless technology that resulted in 4G and 5G systems that transformed the wireless industry.

"What I learned from them was creativity, hard work, and the power of persuasion," Guy recalls. "Number one, the guys were unbelievably creative in trying to solve problems. Number two, they worked around the clock. I was blown away by the fact that even on Sunday, I would be having meetings with them. Much like my father, they taught me that work ethic—because my father was just like that. They taught me that if you have a problem, you do whatever it takes to solve that problem, no matter how long it takes. They did not have a nine-to-five mindset like many of my larger corporate clients."

Another interesting thing Guy observed was how persuasive they were. Here's what Guy says:

> They had an evangelistic spirit and a charisma. I saw firsthand their ability to persuade midlevel executives to pick up everything and move across the United States, risking their careers to go to work for a startup. At that time for those executives, on paper, this was not a good career move. Because in those days, when you were moving up the ladder at Pfizer, you would stay with the company for twenty years, become a VP, and be set for life. If you moved to San Diego and your new company went under, there were hardly any other companies in San Diego where you could have hoped to get a job.

> This gift of being able to persuade people to follow you down an unknown path turns out to be a key trait of great entrepreneurs. Steve Jobs had this in spades, the ability to get people to buy into his vision and to get and keep people excited about an idea because much of the time they are betting their livelihoods on its success.

Qualcomm eventually grew into a multibillion-dollar company, making Jacobs and Viterbi very wealthy. The great thing about the two is that they became major philanthropists. Over the years, Jacobs has contributed hundreds of millions of dollars to education through generous donations and grants to several schools, hospitals, and other local organizations. He gave $31 million to MIT and $250 million to UC San Diego, where he was a professor of computer science and engineering for several years. This was also followed by $100 million to the Salk Institute and $120 million to the San Diego Symphony. For his part, Viterbi made a large donation to his alma mater, and the school of engineering at USC now bears his name.

Once Mentus became known, Guy continued to expand its footprint in biotech and high tech over the years. In 1989, Mentus created the first marketing plan for **CONNECT**, the UCSD program focused on creating an innovation ecosystem replicating the success of Hybritech and Qualcomm for broader-based, high-value-added economic growth in San Diego. In 1992, Guy cofounded **Biocom California**, an organization to accelerate life science throughout the state. The firm provides programs and events that meet the needs of the life sciences community, with a special focus on industry issues, professional development, and networking opportunities.

Mentus, from the beginning, was tasked with promoting and

growing the membership of both CONNECT and Biocom, along with promoting the image of them to their target markets and constituent audiences. Mentus implemented a new brand based on modern elements and applications across all CONNECT and Biocom materials and updated their marketing platforms to expand their reputations. The organizations have both grown to become the largest and most respected regional trade associations in the nation. Biocom has a staff of over a hundred, and nearly two thousand member companies in California and Japan.

In early 2005, the San Diego life science community banded together to respond to the **California Institute for Regenerative Medicine's (CIRM)** request for proposal to solicit bids to build a headquarters site. San Diego's goal was to persuade the CIRM that its facilities and infrastructure made the city the ideal location for the CIRM headquarters, from which $3 billion of stem cell research grants would be administered on a statewide level.

The San Diego team completed a comprehensive written proposal (the design and publishing work courtesy of Mentus) and hosted a site evaluation visit by CIRM representatives. After scoring in the top-three tier following eleven city proposals, the team was invited to make a presentation to the CIRM committee in Sacramento.

Mentus prepared a presentation and was part of the presentation team. San Diego's effort did not result in a winning bid, although CIRM chairman Robert Klein admitted that the San Diego proposal was the most effective and persuasive. Even after Guy's heated arguments with the San Francisco presenter, then-mayor Gavin Newsom, politics still kept it in San Francisco.

Mentus continued to grow by working on the branding and rebranding of dozens of healthcare industry companies, notably market positioning for **HollisterStier** that led to a $129 million acquisition; the rebranding of **Genesis Healthcare** that led to its merger with **Sun Healthcare**; and repositioning **Kite Pharma** that was instrumental in its $12 billion acquisition by Gilead (another Mentus client). In the true spirit of entrepreneurship, Guy diversified Mentus and landed a water conservation campaign for the San Diego Water Authority, the most successful of its kind in California history.

Guy and my late husband, Bud, felt an immediate kinship from the first time they met. They saw something in each other—that they were independent thinkers not bound by the confines of normal expectations but rather by what you can dream and achieve. They met while Bud and I were dating in the 1970s, but it wasn't until the mid-1980s that they worked on a project together.

Bud asked Mentus to brand MB Systems to help garner credibility for the unknown company. While Mentus developed all the sales collateral for the company, it ultimately failed (as discussed in the previous chapter). However, they enjoyed working together. Guy thought of Bud as the brother he never had.

Bud was aware of Guy's extensive knowledge and success and often consulted with him on his many ideas. Bud took Guy's place as a partner on an invitation by the Australian government to evaluate a group of startups in Sydney. Consequently, Bud connected with an Australian innovator who had founded a company Bud helped name: **Injet**. Injet was developing the use of Hewlett-Packard printer technology to distribute a vaporized medicine that would bypass the stomach and go directly into the bloodstream. They moved the company to San Diego, planning to go public and have Bud become its CEO. Mentus became Injet's US marketing agency, and branded the company and its product.

They had several meetings with the Hewlett-Packard team, and they were very close to moving the idea to the next level. However, the founder became distracted by other things, such as studying how long he could extend his life(!) and the stock dilution consequent to an American IPO. The temperament and dysfunctionality of founders can often doom a startup. Once again, that idea didn't work out, and something like a hundred thousand dollars of our money were lost. The only benefit was that Bud got to travel to Australia and scuba dive in the Great Barrier Reef.

Bud and Guy decided to work together on a book that Mentus published called ***The Entrepreneur's Handbook for Raising Capital***. The book focused on how raising capital for an entrepreneur is a life-or-death proposition and details when and how to bring in investors. It breaks down the sources for capital and what a company, big or small, needs to do to access capital. The book also provides a comprehensive list of investment sources, complete with their contact information.

The chapter Bud wrote is entitled "Finding and Keeping the Value in Your Venture." As a consultant, he was an expert at this, but oddly, as an entrepreneur he struggled with it. Guy helped Bud understand that the reason 90 percent of entrepreneurs fail is lack of capital, which was one of Bud's persistent problems with his early ideas.

"The first step is having the idea, but then you have to be able to pay for the second step and then the third step," Guy explains. "Each step in bringing an idea to fruition almost always involves some level of money, and generally the amount of money needed increases with each step."

From his experience with successful entrepreneurs, Guy understood that most successful ventures required complementary partnerships. "Most entrepreneurs, if you look very closely in terms of a particular success, you will find that there's usually one or two people that are intimately involved with the entrepreneur, or they partner together to fill each other's holes," Guy explains. "One handles the money, one handles the creative, one handles the engineering, one handles personnel, and so on."

On his early ideas, Bud never had the right partners or enough money to bring them to fruition. Guy observed that Bud didn't slow down enough to consider the negative side of things. He was always thinking fast and positive. So instead of addressing these deficiencies, he just kept going. That is normal for most entrepreneurs.

"One of the things that he and I talked about is that an entrepreneur will create a company, and a lot of times the company fails on the marketing side," Guy says. "They have a good idea, but they can't get off the ground because no one clearly understands the real value proposition of their product or company."

Guy had developed a workshop that helped senior executives articulate their companies' value proposition and market positioning. Bud internalized this and became very adept at applying this for many of his consulting clients.

The lessons Guy learned from working with successful entrepreneurs like the Hybritech team and Jacobs and Viterbi would prove invaluable to Bud, especially as he approached his final and most successful venture. Guy's understanding of the importance of timing, capital, and partnerships helped shape Bud's approach to what would become his biggest deal. More importantly, Guy's example showed Bud that persistence and adaptability were key traits of successful entrepreneurs.

The relationship between Guy and Bud exemplified how entrepreneurial knowledge and experience can be passed along, shaping and improving others' chances of success. Their story would ultimately influence my decision about how best to honor Bud's legacy—by helping create an educational environment where future entrepreneurs could learn these crucial lessons before embarking on their own ventures.

Guy's work and notoriety landed him on the board of the International Air & Space Hall of Fame. Apparently, he was a mover and shaker in San Diego, but I never had a clear picture of what he was involved with until he invited Bud and me to the induction dinner with five of the surviving Mercury astronauts: Alan Shepard, Scott Carpenter, Gordon Cooper, Wally Schirra, and Deke Slayton. It was a once-in-a-lifetime event and experience.

THE STORY OF THE TILE COMPANY

THE STORY OF THE TILE COMPANY (TTC) represents both Bud's greatest challenges and his ultimate vindication as an entrepreneur. The venture began with his brother Paul, who had moved to Florida in the early 1990s to get into the construction business. Paul started out working at a lumber company and then was hired to run a small retail tile business. At the time, the area had more than fifty carpet stores but only three tile stores. The carpet stores didn't sell tile and vice versa.

Paul's company began importing tile and grew rapidly, as the demand for tile was high but the supply chain lagged. Things changed when large retailers such as Home Depot entered the market and began selling both carpet and tile. As retail became saturated, Paul saw an opening in the wholesale tile business and started TTC. He began purchasing tile from Italy and Spain and selling it to retailers.

TTC grew by doing simple things that competitors weren't doing. The company focused on being a service-driven business. It had an 800 number for retailers, and it opened a large showroom where retailers could view the tile and place orders. Freight was included in the cost of materials, so there were no hidden costs, which were prevalent in the industry.

By 2001, TTC was doing about $40 million a year in sales. It was on solid footing and looking to expand into Georgia and Texas and possibly even build its own manufacturing plant. During a chance dinner on a business trip to Florida, Paul filled Bud in on TTC's burgeoning business. Bud saw an immediate opportunity to take the company public through a reverse merger, a process he had studied extensively during his consulting days.

When the plan was done, Paul discussed it with his two partners. One was in favor, the other against, so Paul cast the deciding vote to move forward. Bud became chairman and began spending his weekdays in Florida, sharing an apartment with one of my cousins who lived there. Having my husband gone five days a week was stressful. In addition to serving as a state representative and working full-time at **Commonfund**, a leading asset management firm, I was raising three children. But Bud was convinced this was a big opportunity.

Bud put together an ambitious pitch deck for a vertically integrated tile company. It would have four primary areas of business: tile manufacturing (they were looking into building a plant instead of just importing), retail floor covering stores (selling carpet, natural stone, porcelain tile, vinyl flooring, and prefinished hardwood flooring), tile wholesale distribution (to larger stores and contractors), and online sales (through a license to a kiosk-based marketing system to be sublicensed to building material sales websites).

Going public at that time was much easier than it is today, particularly for a small business. The initial goal was to reach $100 million in sales, deemed a magic number to take TTC public through a reverse merger. The company increased its sales to about $75 million. Though this was short of the $100 million, Bud was still able to take TTC public through a reverse merger with a company called Terra. The transaction ended up costing about $1.5 million, not a huge sum for such a deal but a sizeable one for the cash-strapped, newly minted TTC Terra.

The stock struggled to gain traction from the start. It was first listed on the **over-the-counter (OTC) exchange**, which is for securities that are not listed on a major stock exchange and are traded in a broker-dealer network because most are small companies that don't meet the requirements to be traded on larger exchanges. Bud then moved the stock to the Alternative Investment Market (AIM) in London, the British version of the OTC, but it continued to fight trading headwinds. The company's balance sheet simply wasn't strong enough to attract buyers.

Then in 2002, everything changed. With the passage of the Sarbanes–Oxley Act, the US Congress tightened regulations on public companies, to protect shareholders from fraudulent accounting practices in the wake of massive accounting scandals at Enron and WorldCom. Compliance costs for public companies shot up, and the bill disproportionally affected smaller companies. TTC Terra had budgeted $600,000 a year for accounting and regulatory costs, but that number ballooned to $2 million.

Even though the stock was going nowhere, the business itself was able to support those costs until the bottom fell out of the construction industry heading into the 2008 housing market crisis. TTC Terra had $30 million in assets and inventory that it couldn't move and $40 million in debt. Bank of America, which was owed $17 million, took over the company and sold the assets to a hedge fund for $10 million, or twenty cents on the dollar. All that was left was what is known as a non-reporting public company, with no operating business.

Bud was incredibly upset but also embarrassed because all the investors they had brought in, including my brother Guy, lost their money. Looking for a way to make his investors whole, Bud decided to retain the non-reporting public company, which had three hundred original restricted shareholders from when the company went public. He renamed it Terra Enterprises, Inc.

While Bud was looking for a company to do a reverse merger with, he found a small retail company called **Covering and Tile Flooring**. The company was run by a well-regarded man who had accumulated $86,000 of debt. Bud made a deal to purchase Covering and Tile Flooring, and I helped him pay off the debt with money from my meager retirement fund, producing yet another source of anxiety for me.

For the next ten years, Bud ran Covering and Tile Flooring, basically doing every job. He was stocking the store, selling the tile and carpeting to customers, supervising installations, doing all the bookkeeping, and keeping the entity going as a public company. There was such a disconnect between the actual business and its position as a publicly traded company that the stock went from being a penny stock to a 1/1000 of a penny stock. Bud was constantly trying to grow the business to increase the stock price, but it was a real struggle.

Though this small retail store was doing around $700,000 a year in business, expenses were so high that Bud didn't take a salary. He had showroom, storage facility, and insurance bills, along with having to deal with price fluctuations of the materials. But people loved working with him because he ran an honest business and put his customers first, and they were constantly referring business to him.

While running the day-to-day operations at Covering and Tile Flooring, Bud was continually trying to merge Terra with another company that was related to the housing renovation or construction business or to find a buyer for the company. He had many conversations with companies, and a few of them bought the stock because it was so cheap. Bud was so sure that he would find a deal that, unbeknownst to me, he continued to buy a large number of shares of the stock on the open market. At $0.001, that meant one million shares cost all of $1,000.

I later learned that he could have cashed out big time but didn't because of me. One of his contacts in the OTC trading business approached him about selling Terra to a marijuana company looking to go public. Their pitch was that the deal could have an upside of $100 million once marijuana was legalized. Bud told them that he couldn't do it, or I would divorce him. I was so totally opposed to legalizing marijuana in any form and had spent years in the legislature battling against legalization.

On the rumor of the marijuana deal, Terra stock jumped from the fractions of a cent range to ten cents a share. But once the small market of penny stock traders got wind that Bud would not do the marijuana deal, the stock plummeted to its lowest of low points, something like $0.00001 a share.

All of this was difficult for Bud to handle. It was very stressful, and I could tell it was taking a toll on him. The fun-loving, free-spirited guy became a serious, contemplative guy. There were times when I would wake up in the middle of the night and find him sitting on the edge of the bed with his head in his hands. He was always one step away from being forced to shut the whole thing down, but he couldn't let himself.

Heading into the fall of 2020, Bud had spent ten stressful years and untold thousands of dollars in regulatory fees while looking for another company to buy the publicly traded company or merge with it. At our fiftieth wedding anniversary dinner, he told me that if he couldn't find a partner to do a deal for Terra, he would shut it down at the end of December but keep Covering and Tile Flooring going, as the business gave him great joy.

What he hadn't told me was that in 2019, a month after our anniversary and just before he planned to shut down his publicly traded company, he had been approached by **XChange**, a fintech company that was looking for the shortest and easiest route to go public. The company was based on the West Coast, so Bud had asked my brother to look into them. Guy dug around and found out they had been around for years, were on solid footing, but maintained a very low profile.

XChange clearly had nothing to do with the flooring industry, but that was beside the point. The main concern was that they were considering three companies to merge with, so Terra could easily lose out. There was a lot of back-and-forth between Bud and XChange's team over the outstanding numbers of shares and which of the outstanding shares needed to be canceled to complete the transaction. It was a very complex deal, done behind the scenes, that I knew nothing about.

The upshot was that the deal happened. In the fall of 2020, XChange purchased Terra for a five-figure promissory note at $0.00001 a share. Bud called it "a business miracle." I had never seen a bigger smile on his face or the sense of satisfaction he felt. He would have to wait ninety days to sell the stock he had accumulated on the open market to realize any monetary gain.

He came home the day after the deal closed and disclosed to me what had happened for the first time. He said, "Toni, you know how you're always worried we're going to lose everything? If this stock only goes to fifty cents, we're going to be good." He put his arm around my shoulder, adding, "Trust me, it's going to be good."

Toni and Bud Boucher

Just as Bud predicted, the stock began to take off. It went to a penny, then three cents, then ten cents, then twenty cents. By the end of the year, it closed at eighty-four cents per share—an 84,000 percent increase! Everything Bud had hoped for was lining up to come true. His shares were now worth millions of dollars—if only he could have lived long enough to sell them.

But fate had other plans. A month and a half after the deal closed, Bud was diagnosed with a rare form of leukemia. Though he remained upbeat about his treatment and the prospects for the stock, his condition deteriorated rapidly. He passed away just weeks before the restricted period on selling his shares would expire, leaving me to navigate both grief and the complex process of realizing his final triumph.

His journey exemplified both the promise and perils of entrepreneurship. He had incredible vision and persistence, but often lacked the right partners or sufficient capital to bring his ideas to fruition. His story would ultimately inspire an investment in helping future entrepreneurs avoid these pitfalls and find success through proper education and support. But first, I had to figure out how to fulfill his final vision.

THE STORY OF THE TILE COMPANY   57

6 REALIZING A LEGACY

THE WEEKS FOLLOWING BUD'S DEATH were an emotional roller coaster. While still in a state of shock, I found myself scrambling to keep Covering and Tile Flooring going, as the company was in the middle of installing flooring in a sixty-five-unit condo building. I was also preparing to sell the stock in the company that had pushed Bud to his limits while I was still working for Commonfund. I was determined not to let Bud down, to realize his dream of providing financial security for our family and to do some good with whatever money was left over. Though I had no idea how many obstacles were in my way and how many hurdles I would have to jump, I knew it would be hard to go through this without my partner who had been by my side for fifty-five years.

Before any of Bud's dreams could be realized, I had to navigate a maze of financial and legal obstacles that seemed insurmountable. Although I was still in state of shock and grief, immediately after his death, I started by calling our estate attorney about having Bud's will go through probate so I could take possession of the stock. She told me that probate could take months. "I'm going to give you just one thing to do every single day because I know you can't emotionally handle more," she said. "But you can't do a thing with the stock until the probate court gives you full legal authority."

She promised to use every tool in her bag to get the probate done quickly. By some stroke of luck, or perhaps divine intervention, the court turned it around in twenty-four hours. She said that in the history of her career, she had never had a turnover that fast.

The next problem was finding the accounts where the stock was parked so that I could begin selling it when it became possible. Bud had three brokerage accounts at major firms. I found a statement for the first brokerage firm and called them.

The broker said he would check with his compliance department. He called back and told me that his compliance officer said I was an "affiliate" (because we owned a significant number of shares). As such, because there was so much outstanding stock, I could not sell the shares. He also told me that Terra had never filed with the SEC and was therefore not in compliance.

I couldn't believe what I was hearing. He was telling me that Bud had sold a publicly traded company legally but did not file the proper paperwork. Who would buy such a company? I knew this couldn't be right.

I found the phone number of the XChange attorney on the paperwork and called him to find out who Bud's CFO was. I called the CFO and explained that, according to my broker, the stock was not in compliance with SEC regulations.

He explained that the broker was wrong. Penny stock companies were exempt from filing with the SEC. Instead, they had to file with Financial Industry Regulatory Authority (FINRA), a private corporation that self-regulates brokerage firms and exchange markets for penny stocks. Terra had done that, so he sent me all of the filings.

I next called the stock transfer agent and told her what the broker had said about my being restricted from selling the stock because I was an affiliate. She told me they were incorrect. To make the deal go through, Bud had canceled enough shares so that he was no longer an affiliate (which meant I wasn't) and was therefore allowed to sell stock he had purchased years before on the open market.

This very large and prestigious brokerage firm had been dead wrong on two counts! I told them that I was transferring everything I had to another firm.

At this point, I found that Bud had also purchased shares on the open market that were in his IRA at a second top brokerage firm. I called them to prepare to sell those shares and hit another brick wall.

The broker told me that they did not have a digital record of the trade, which had been made in December of 2010, because they did not keep those records in their computer system after seven years. I would need to provide them with that statement or wait for him to send a request to their archives for a paper copy. That process would take many months, time that I did not have. The process was a race against the clock. XChange was making some business moves, and the stock began running up, passing $1 a share in late January on its way to closing at more than $5 in early February. I knew in my gut it couldn't possibly last. I had to find this trade confirmation, which was somewhere in the thousands of files Bud kept.

So now I was really tortured. Bud's files were a mess. None of them were chronological, and they contained everything he had ever been involved in. He was treasurer of the Rotary Club, treasurer of the American Legion Veterans, treasurer of the Knights of Columbus, and treasurer of Teen Center Board in Wilton. He had multiple files for all of these, in addition to his accounts receivable and business files for Terra and for Covering and Tile Flooring and other ventures.

I spread the boxes upon boxes of files out on my bedroom floor and started to go through each file, page by page. I bought thirty plastic crates at Staples to organize them. I literally couldn't walk across the room without stepping on a stack of papers or tripping on a plastic crate.

Reading the files, I learned the full extent of his struggle to sell. There were a series of nondisclosure records from merger possibilities. I found emails from a consultant for OTC publicly traded companies that had introduced Bud to XChange. The consultant had repeatedly expressed concern that Terra had too much outstanding stock and that the other two companies he had recommended had a better chance of making a deal with XChange.

Taking those remarks seriously, Bud had canceled enough shares of outstanding stock through his transfer agent to make the deal more attractive. As president, he could issue shares of stock and also cancel them. He had decided to give XChange the best financial deal he could devise. I also saw that Bud had engaged in multiple conversations and emails with XChange's founder, who said that he liked Bud's financial acumen, integrity, and concern for his own shareholders. In the end, Bud had offered him Terra for a modest promissory note issued by XChange, and the deal had closed.

After two days of searching, I was exhausted. I had barely slept. I felt like I was looking for a needle in a haystack, but I pressed on. I pulled what felt like a desperation all-nighter. Around 6 a.m., after hours of searching, I started to sob. In frustration, I plunged my hand into a crate and pulled out a random piece of paper. And there it was: the trade confirmation from December 2010, confirming the purchase of the shares on the open market.

If what had happened in the fall was a miracle, this was a second one.

I knew I had the critical document, but by this point I was numb. First thing in the morning, I called the broker at the firm that held the IRA. He was as surprised as I was. The good news, he said, was that I could trade the shares. The bad news was that the shares hadn't averaged more than $5 a share over the previous twelve months, and due to their company's policy, they could not sell any of the shares.

I called a third major firm where Bud had multiple accounts, including an IRA. I spoke to the broker who had opened the account for Bud, which he had done in anticipation of placing the stock there to sell. The broker told me that if I could have the stock transferred to his firm, he would sell all the shares.

So that's what I did. Through a contact at the firm holding the IRA, we persuaded them to transfer the stock. The broker at that firm that was now holding all the stocks introduced me to their top trader on the block desk. The trader was deeply affected by my story. It turned out his wife was going through cancer treatment, and we immediately established a bond. As soon as the restriction ended, I started selling the stock with this trader. We did this over a period of time because the stock price was so fragile, and I didn't want it to collapse and harm other shareholders' opportunities.

As I had feared, the stock price didn't hold, and I never captured it at the highest point, but that didn't matter. I had so many shares that Bud had purchased at a fraction of a cent that the amounts I realized did far more than enough to make us alright, just as he had promised.

I had encountered every conceivable obstacle: legal, brokerage, compliance, you name it. But somehow through divine intervention, I was able to circumvent all of them and end up with a stock-trading case for the history books—not from the actual dollar amount realized but by the velocity of speed at which shares that had been worth less than nothing became such a sizable amount in record time.

Here is what is even more remarkable. On paper, Bud had drawn in pencil the entire chart of how this was going to play out. A line graph of the stock went up and to the right, landing at almost the exact high. Even more extraordinary is that he had been one month away from shutting the whole thing down.

Bud did get to enjoy seeing a couple people who believed in him reap the rewards when the deal originally closed in the fall of 2020. One of them was a friend who owned a garage door company in the area. Bud had encouraged him to buy the stock when it was a fraction of a cent, so he bought several thousand dollars worth.

After the XChange deal closed and the stock began to rise, Bud got a phone call from his friend. He told Bud he was driving his son to soccer practice when he received a call from his broker, who explained that his account was being transferred to the high-net-worth department. The guy was confused. The broker asked if he had seen what was going on with Terra stock. He said that he hadn't looked at it in years. The broker laughed and told him that his stock was now worth a few million dollars. He nearly drove off the road.

"You've changed my family's life forever, and I don't know how to thank you," he told Bud.

For Bud, that was thanks enough. He felt so good that his friends who had believed in him were reaping the benefits of his long journey.

A year after Bud died, a friend emailed me and told me an amazing story of how Bud had changed her life. She explained that she had waited to reach out to me, out of consideration for my grief. She had worked on my gubernatorial exploratory campaign, and she and Bud had belonged to a business networking group that provided members referrals and leads. When it was Bud's turn to talk about his business, he told them that they all knew he had a retail flooring business, but what they didn't know was that it was a part of a publicly traded company, Terra Enterprises, Inc. "The cost of the stock is very inexpensive," he told them. "I have plans to grow it, and I encourage you to buy some stock."

Very few people took him up on his offer. But they had become friends, and she thought highly enough of him to take a chance. She invested all that she had in her brokerage account, some $6,000, and had all but forgotten about the investment until she read Bud's obituary in the paper. She then checked her account. Her shares had grown, and her account was worth several million dollars. She thought the firm had made a mistake, so she called her broker. He assured her there was no mistake, and she sold all her stock that very day.

It was yet another miracle in many ways. Only eight months prior, she had buried her disabled sister, who she had lived with and taken care of for many years. Her bookkeeping business had suffered as a result. The house they had always lived in was in foreclosure. To make matters worse, her small cabin in the Tennessee mountains had been burned by a fire, and she had no money to fix it. But now her world had changed in an instant.

All her financial problems had disappeared in one day. She paid off her mortgage, fixed the mountain cabin, and bought a luxury high-rise apartment.

She told me that she also invited her brother and friends to the New York Yankees and Rangers games with her new season tickets. The only requirement, she said, was that at the end of every game, they had to look up at the sky and say, "Thank you, Bud!"

7 YOU GET WHAT YOU GIVE

WHEN BUD SOLD TERRA, he knew what he had accomplished. He was so much more optimistic than me about what the outcome would be. I thought the company that bought Terra would fail in three months or even sooner, and we would never see a dime. He was so confident that he asked me, "What do you want to do philanthropically? Who do you want to help?" He said, "Johns Hopkins Medical Center? My school, Saint Michael's College? Our children's, Georgetown University? Yours, UConn? The Town of Wilton's nonprofits?"

I said, "All of them and more, but first UConn."

I told him I wanted to do more for **UConn** because it was our state university and because their business school had been so flexible when I was trying to cobble together my MBA while serving in the legislature, working full-time at **Commonfund**, and raising three children who were about to go to college. At the time, there had been a requirement to complete your MBA by the four-year deadline, but when I explained my dilemma to UConn business school leadership, they extended the deadline multiple times. I felt UConn really cared about me and how I was trying to juggle my courses, my investment job, and public service work while raising three children. They wanted me to succeed, and I felt a deep desire to pay them back.

In 2004, we had taken a baby step. I created a fund that supported UConn's business school and the **Toni Boucher Scholarship** that gave financial stipends to incoming students in need. I had told Michael Van Sambeck, who was the head of development for the business school, that one day I hoped to do more if Bud's company did better in the future. I had known Michael for years from his time working as a staffer in the state senate and held him in high regard.

Our family also had a positive history with UConn. My first cousin Nicholas Iannuzzi, who came to America with only a rudimentary elementary school education, had worked his way to UConn through junior colleges and graduated in 1951 in the first class of the physical therapy program. Bud's brother Dennis—a retired Army Ranger Lt. Colonel who served at the Pentagon—and his wife, Diane, met at and graduated from UConn. Most recently, our nephew had graduated from the engineering school.

So, after Bud passed away and I realized the financial miracle that he had created, my goal was to give as little as I could to taxes and as much as I could to philanthropy. Having served in government much of my adult life, I knew how much more productive it was to give to nonprofit organizations like UConn than to the federal and state treasuries.

I called Michael and told him that the day I hoped for had come. I could do more for UConn. Over the winter of 2022, Michael and I began a larger conversation over many lunches and dinners about what the business school needed to take it to the next level. We discussed how I could build a lasting legacy to Bud through a gift that would enhance the dreams of the school's budding entrepreneurs. These conversations narrowed my focus to UConn's School of Business Management & Entrepreneurship Department.

Michael Van Sambeck and Toni Boucher enjoying UConn's Final Four run.

As I mentioned in the prologue, the state of Connecticut has long been known as the birthplace of invention and innovation since early colonial times and as the marketplace of the original thirteen colonies. I felt that a focus on education and research could ignite new ideas and new solutions. It could invigorate the entrepreneurial spirit across all departments at UConn and extend throughout the state over time. The mission would be to help transform these new ideas into new companies that could grow jobs and provide opportunities to all levels of the economy.

Heading into 2020, UConn was recognized as a top-twenty-five business school among public research institutions. The next step would be to move the university into the top ten, joining Ross School of Business at the University of Michigan, Kenan-Flagler Business School at the University of North Carolina, and McCombs School of Business at the University of Texas at Austin. To achieve this, UConn was looking to strengthen its faculty, to attract the best possible students, and to provide those students with opportunities to become the innovators and business leaders of tomorrow.

Several things stood out. Student demand for entrepreneurship education rose 66 percent during the first two years of the COVID-19 pandemic, according to the UConn School of Business. UConn, as a land-grant university, has an obligation to make its research have an economic impact on the state, and entrepreneurship is a key vehicle that can help fulfill that responsibility.

Over the past decade, UConn's **Management & Entrepreneurship Department** and its campus partners such as the **Connecticut Center for Entrepreneurship and Innovation (CCEI)** and the **Peter J. Werth Institute for Entrepreneurship and Innovation** have helped students engage in entrepreneurial activities and have helped launch numerous companies. These successful founders learned and developed alongside thousands of other students, alumni, and community members in UConn experiential learning activities and venture development initiatives, such as the **Innovation Quest**, the **Wolff New Venture Competition**, the **Get Seeded** program, and other beneficial incubators on campus. (In 2025, two startups that utilized seed stage financing and business development support from the Wolff New Venture Competition and other CCEI programs have recently achieved major success milestones. Phoenix Tailings recently closed a $43 million in funding, while Veradermics raised $75 million.)

I saw my gift as an enhancement of these programs and a way to move the M&E Department to the next level, expand venture education and employment opportunities for students, and enable the department to respond to shifts in the marketplace to meet the future needs of employers. Specifically, it would fund three distinct programs to advance UConn's role as a leader in entrepreneurship.

Toni Boucher is committed to making UConn one of the top business schools in the nation and the home to many future entrepreneurs.

First, it would create a new technology commercialization venture fund that would allow students to learn how to assess the commercial portfolios of technologies, to identify investors most likely to succeed, and to make financial investments in existing startups as a way to simulate the actual investing process. In conjunction with this hands-on learning, the M&E Department would also create new classes focused on tech commercialization.

Second, it would provide direct support to those inventors and scientists with viable ideas by creating a founder "boot camp" to assist entrepreneurs in commercializing their inventions.

Third, it would provide immersive education in tech commercialization by allowing students to visit existing companies and examine their operations so that they could better understand how to think like entrepreneurs.

8 THE ENTREPRENEURSHIP ECOSYSTEM

DURING THE TALKS, I met with **Dean John Elliott** and **Dr. Greg Reilly**, head of the Management and Entrepreneurship Department and a tenured professor with impeccable credentials and a personality to match. I also became friends with **UConn president Radenka Maric**. As noted in an earlier chapter, before coming to UConn as a professor, she was a successful entrepreneur in her own right. She served as vice president for research and innovation before being elevated to university president.

When I explained my goal to Greg in our first meeting, he summed it up perfectly: "You want to help turn innovations and inventions into thriving businesses, thereby creating jobs."

The talks culminated in February of 2022 when I pledged a gift of $8 million to name the **Boucher Management & Entrepreneurship Department** in the UConn School of Business. It was the largest gift that the business school had ever received for a department. The gift, or investment as I liked to call it, would double the teaching capacity of the new student venture fund program, and provide flexible resources to pilot new programs that will prepare students for the jobs and business challenges of tomorrow.

Dean Elliott saw the gift as an expansion of the university's mission. "Naming the Boucher Department of Management & Entrepreneurship was a fundamental transformation in acknowledging the importance of entrepreneurship at the university," he said.

My husband was my greatest example, next to my father, of never giving up on yourself when all others give up on you, proving that dogged determination can lead to success. He never gave up, even after countless failures. He picked himself up, dusted himself off, and forged ahead. This was the motivation behind my investment in UConn—that its students and educators would be encouraged to not be afraid to fail, that failure is part of the learning process, and that they will be supported on their entrepreneurial journey.

We had discussions about broader issues, such as social justice and creating more fairness and equity in the economic landscape of our state and our country. I told them that for me, the best social justice program is creating job opportunities for everyone at every level so that they can elevate and better their lives and, in turn, improve the communities where they live.

The business school wanted to bring together a lot of different programs on entrepreneurship, and do it in a way that could extend these courses to students from all different disciplines. Whether it would lead to an MBA or not, the students could learn how to take an idea from just an idea to fruition—and my, how a young Bud would've loved to learn that!

If Bud had had that tool, he would've been so much further ahead. But his approach was hitting his head against the wall time after time. He didn't do self-reflection. Had he done that, he could have rebooted some of his ideas by updating the model and figuring out how to make it work. Now, through this gift, future entrepreneurs would have the support system Bud never had, learning from both successes and failures in a structured environment designed to help them succeed.

The engine driving the Boucher Management & Entrepreneurship Department is Greg Reilly, a former entrepreneur whose own journey to academia uniquely qualifies him to bridge the gap between theory and practice. After earning his bachelor's degree from the **University of Michigan**, where his roommate was Tony Fadell (who would later become known as the "father of the iPod"), Greg went to Silicon Valley in the early days of the internet. He worked to put banking balances and transfers online for Wells Fargo and Bank of America, but eventually returned to Michigan to pursue his own entrepreneurial path.

In 1997, he started a company called Measure.net, based on the idea that companies were too focused on measuring what they could measure instead of measuring what they wanted to know. Measure.net flipped that on its head by helping corporate leadership teams focus on what would be most important to know based on their strategy, and then figuring out how to measure that.

When the dot-com bubble burst following 9/11, Greg made a pivot that would ultimately benefit countless future entrepreneurs—he earned his PhD at the University of Wisconsin. Getting a PhD while he and his wife juggled caring for four kids under six years old gives you some idea of his energy level and persistence. He then applied to several business schools as an assistant professor and was hired by UConn in 2007, the first academic job he had ever held.

"I had no ties to Connecticut at that time, but now it's the place I've lived the longest, and there is no place else I would rather live," he proclaims.

While creating and running the graduate program in Human Resources, he rose from assistant professor to associate professor and earned tenure. In 2019, he was promoted to professor and was named department head of the M&E program. One of his early goals was to position the department nationally to attract top talent to UConn to study and teach entrepreneurship, and to grow the reputation of the UConn School of Business.

Greg's approach to teaching entrepreneurship is far from traditional:

> People learn when their belief structures are challenged and fail. When we are forced to confront our own models of the world, and then we try to apply our model of the world and we fail, we step back and say, "Oh, my way of thinking falls short in this situation." And now the instructor is there with an alternative idea to try, not to say "I have the answer" but to say "Why don't you think about a tweak on the way you are thinking, update your model, and try it differently?" That's how people learn. I always push people to write what they think, make a prediction, confront the reality of the result, and then give them an opportunity to update their model. All of this takes a ton of self-reflection, but thinking about how you think is vital.

His wife, Judith, must have been paying attention, as she also launched an innovative new program that is catching fire throughout the country as executive director of the university's Center for Neurodiversity and Employment.

Dr. Greg Reilly, head of the Boucher Management and Entrepreneurship Department in the UConn School of Business

One of the department's most innovative additions is Dr. Ryan Coles, who joined UConn in 2020 after completing his PhD at Cornell University. His specialty in international entrepreneurship has brought a global perspective to the program. As chief scientist of the **Jamie and Kyle Daigle Lab for Applied Entrepreneurship Research (Daigle Labs)**, Ryan conducts rigorous research on how businesses are built and founded, then applies these insights to help commercialize new technology.

The genesis of **Daigle Labs** itself demonstrates the entrepreneurial spirit it studies. The seed funding for the lab came from Kyle Daigle, the COO of GitHub, a developer platform that is now part of Microsoft. During the COVID-19 pandemic, Ryan was running in his neighborhood when he passed a house with the newest Tesla solar panels. The owner, Kyle Daigle, was in the yard, and Ryan stopped to ask about the panels.

Dr. Ryan Coles, chief scientist at Daigle Labs

From there, the two struck up a friendship. They found they had similar beliefs about entrepreneurship, how it can be taught and learned. Oddly enough, Kyle was in the process of getting an online undergraduate degree from UConn during the pandemic, as he had dropped out of Boston University years earlier to work at GitHub. But even though he had established himself as a prominent tech executive, nobody in the business school knew he was a UConn alum, because he had gotten his degree online at age thirty-two.

The lab's structure itself is innovative compared to how academic labs are typically funded. Rather than relying solely on grants or endowment funding, Ryan's goal is to create a third revenue stream by commercializing the lab's research. In 2023, Ryan and the Daigle Labs team accepted or initiated eight startup projects commercializing research in the AI, energy, biomaterials, agriculture, and aerospace sectors. Over that period,

Daigle Labs oversaw millions in new sales contracts. Though the liquidation events at these companies will take time, ultimately there will be a return to the lab for its contribution.

The lab pursues opportunities everywhere in the world, from major US cities to Latin American countries with a history of drug cartel violence, from the Amazon rainforest to agrarian Bedouin communities in the Middle East. They even found one at the top of the Himalayas, where they traveled in 2020 to help Yak Cheese, a local purveyor of cheese that it wanted to export.

This unique project started when Ryan received an email from Peter Werth, who was working with a cheese factory in one of the most remote human villages in the world, located in the Upper Dolpo region of Nepal. To get to Yak Cheese, Ryan and his student, John Hiden, had to hike up to over 17,000 feet.

"It's important to realize that businesses are everywhere," Hiden explains. "I think when we talk about entrepreneurship, I hope the conversation is able to switch away from just billion-dollar companies to facilitating real economic development using entrepreneurship in remote areas, in developing areas, because that is just as important as Apple or Google."

The department has also initiated activities so that students can implement their assumptions and figure out how to make changes in real time. One of its signature programs is a **Leveraged Buyout (LBO)** competition that started in 2023 and is capably led by Assistant Professor Sami Ghaddar.

In the LBO competition, students form teams, pick out a target company, and do the due diligence from an LBO perspective, both on investment thesis and rationale. They complete a full-fledged LBO model and figure out the internal rate of return and what the multiple will be on invested capital. The teams work with one of ten alumni advisors on developing a proposal to execute the transaction. After two rounds of cuts, the finalists go to New York for a live session to determine which one did the best analysis and proposal for an LBO.

The judges for the competition are experienced businesspeople who work in the LBO world, and they push the students pretty hard—just like they would push their own employees when they are spending millions and even hundreds of millions of dollars of their company's money. These interactions with experts in the LBO field are better than anything the students could learn in a classroom or a case study, and to top it off, the winning team receives a cash prize that they can put toward their tuition.

Another innovative program now under the Boucher Management & Entrepreneurship Department is **Innovation Quest**, known as **iQ**. Although the program is a part of the business school, all UConn undergraduate and graduate students can participate. One of the great advantages of the iQ competition is that it welcomes all ideas, be they software or medical devices, engineering technology, or a needed consumer product.

Each entering participant completes four workshops in February and March and then submits a formal application with their business idea. A panel of judges selects the most promising enterprises in April. Those teams then compete for $30,000 in startup funds and a chance to attend the university's Summer InQbator, a next-step entrepreneurship boot camp.

After more than a decade under the guidance of Professor Rich Dino, the iQ program is now led by Kevin Gardiner, an MBA graduate of UConn and an adjunct professor in both the School of Business and College of Engineering. Kevin has served as an iQ mentor for several years and has held management and senior management positions at both startups and stalwarts, including Welcome Commerce, Macy's, and Oracle. His advice to the budding entrepreneurs: build a strong team.

"Most people think that a good idea and a million bucks will make a company soar, but that's only a piece of the puzzle," Kevin says. "I would bet on an A-Team with a B-Idea, over a B-Team with an A-Idea every time."

The success stories from these programs demonstrate their impact. Consider Amelia Martin, an undergraduate student who developed Mud Rat, a company making sustainable surfboards with cores made from mycelium, the underground root-like structure of fungi. She entered her idea in iQ to gain business knowledge, test it out, and meet advisers who could help her bring it to fruition.

The transformative power of the department's programs is perhaps best illustrated by the story of Joseph Roberts. Growing up in a rough area of New Haven, Joseph's path to UConn was anything but traditional. His parents did not attend college, and his high school didn't provide the necessary resources for higher education. He graduated with a barely passable 1.6 GPA and took jobs working the graveyard shift in stock rooms at Walmart and Target.

Unsatisfied with his direction in life, he pivoted to get his Certified Nursing Assistant (CNA) license and began traveling around Connecticut helping elderly individuals with their daily living needs. When COVID-19 hit in 2020 and made it hard for CNAs to remain in homes, he began to rethink his goals.

"I sat back and said, 'Yasir—which is my middle name—you have to get it together and find something you are passionate about,'" he recalls. "I decided to try finance, which I had always been interested in, and I enrolled at Gateway Community College in New Haven."

After two strong academic years at Gateway, he discovered **Hillside Ventures,** a student-run investment firm (more on this in the next chapter), through its website and decided to enroll at UConn. In August of 2022, he was accepted and joined Hillside's sustainability vertical, where he amazingly rose to become its leader.

Under his leadership, the vertical made five investments. Joseph found one of those investments, Voltpost, at an entrepreneurship conference in Boston. Voltpost is an electric vehicle charging platform that retrofits lampposts into high-speed charging stations that have twenty feet of retractable cable and can accommodate two to four charging ports. Since the Hillside investment, Voltpost has executed on its promise, expanding operations from New York to Chicago, San Francisco, and Detroit, and closing a further $3.6 million round of seed funding in July 2023.

Another success story is that of Aria Penna, who credits the Werth Institute and Hillside with changing her entire focus from law to business. She was originally enrolled in a fast-track law degree program but pivoted to business because of the hands-on opportunities.

The switch paid off. She became so involved in Hillside that she ended up working on the most deals that were completed in her three years there, and she also constructed a plan to broaden recruiting across campus. Her experience with Hillside was a key factor in her landing a plum internship as an investment banking analyst at Citibank's New York headquarters, which ultimately led to a job offer.

"Hillside Ventures has been invaluable for my own professional development and growth within UConn and has really set me up for the career I want," she says. "Getting those reps all the way from initially sourcing a company to writing a one-pager to the full memo creation and really understanding that process and how to interface with the investment board has made all the difference."

Business student Aria Penna is one of the success stories in UConn's program.

The students in these programs have thoroughly impressed me with their increasing confidence and capabilities. I've watched them in the classroom debating with one another and with Greg on investments, and I've seen firsthand their growing self-assurance. I was elated to hear them describe their participation in a student-run investment conference with their counterparts from Harvard. They talked about how they entered the room with a sense of intimidation and left the program with a sense of pride and self-confidence, feeling that they were just as good as the Harvard students.

The department's impact extends far beyond individual success stories. The multidisciplinary approach to entrepreneurship education has attracted increased involvement from successful alumni, who see in these programs the kind of practical education they wish they'd had access to during their college years.

The focus is increasingly on "doing" rather than just learning. This hands-on approach was pioneered when alum Keith Fox, a former senior executive at Apple and Cisco, started the UConn Innovation Quest competition in 2012. The competition is extracurricular, and students don't receive academic credit. They work on their idea and present it to a panel of judges. The winning organizations then have the ability to start a company with funds awarded by the judges.

The next step in the department's evolution came with adding a STEM vertical to its programs in fall 2022. This initiative is unique in that it draws students primarily from outside the business school, including music majors and physics majors.

A real estate investment experiential program, backed by alum Jim Whalen of TA Realty, gives students hands-on experience in commercial real estate ventures.

In January of 2024, Greg launched an adjunct program called **Hillside Private Capital.** This program provides students with the opportunity to collaborate with leading asset managers, blending educational sessions with real-world financial analysis. The program involves both in-person and virtual sessions hosted by professionals to study private asset classes and explore investment and asset management strategies.

UConn alum Debra Hess, whose career as a CFO spans several investment firms, was able to set up a collaboration with the Fortress Investment Group, a leading global investment manager with some $48 billion under management. This was a major coup because UConn became the first university partnered with a major Wall Street private equity firm that allows students to shadow investment professionals working on deals in progress.

The department has also recognized that all of these ventures need proper marketing and brand development to succeed. Working with mentors from successful companies, students learn how to position their ideas and communicate their value proposition effectively. This includes understanding social media strategy, content marketing, and how to build relationships with potential customers and investors.

"We keep coming back to the most important thing," Greg says, "which is that as you learn here, it's not about the results, because this is the students' learning laboratory; it's their place to take chances. We flip the priority, we take the risks, and we make mistakes because that's how we learn."

The success of these programs has helped elevate UConn's standing in entrepreneurship education. Five years ago, the entrepreneurship programs were unranked by the Princeton Review. By 2024, they had risen to forty-first in undergraduate rankings and twenty-eighth in graduate school rankings.

Perhaps more importantly, these programs are changing how students think about business and their role in creating positive change in the world. The department's approach emphasizes that entrepreneurship isn't just about starting companies—it's about solving problems, creating value, and making a positive impact on society.

This philosophical shift is particularly evident in the department's focus on social entrepreneurship. Students are encouraged to think about how their ventures can address social and environmental challenges while building sustainable businesses. This aligns with the changing priorities of today's students, who increasingly seek purpose-driven careers.

The transformation of the department under the Boucher name represents more than just a change in title—it represents a fundamental shift in how entrepreneurship is taught and practiced. By combining rigorous academic study with practical experience and emphasizing both the business and human aspects of entrepreneurship, the department is creating a new model for entrepreneurship education that would have given someone like Bud the tools he needed to succeed much earlier in his journey.

INVESTING IN TOMORROW

Venture capital is the lifeblood of entrepreneurs. The concept was invented by Georges Doriot, dubbed "the father of venture capitalism," to encourage private investment in businesses started by soldiers who had returned from World War II. Since then, venture capital, now known as VC, has gone through many incarnations.

The first boom for VC was in the late 1970s and early 1980s when startup companies like Apple, FedEx, and Microsoft sought to raise capital to grow their businesses prior to going public. As these companies' values rose exponentially by the time they did go public, this showed that first dollars invested at an early stage of a good idea could result in massive financial gains.

At the heart of UConn's experiential learning in entrepreneurship is a $1 million student-run venture capital fund, mentioned in the previous chapter, that is revolutionizing how students learn about investment and entrepreneurship: **Hillside Ventures**. Like many great entrepreneurial stories, Hillside's origin comes from a student seeing an opportunity. Noah Sobel-Pressman conceived the idea in his freshman year after seeing a LinkedIn post about a similar fund at Ohio's Miami University.

Working with **David Noble**, director of the **Werth Institute**, Noah spent his sophomore year as a Werth Innovator and did an internship with Techstars. Seven other Werth students also had significant internships in areas related to venture capital and investing. This led to the creation of an independent study, led by David in the spring of 2019, on how to create a venture fund for students to make investments, how to raise the money, and how to find experienced partners to participate.

As part of that study, Noah and his fellow students invited asset allocators, lawyers, and accountants to campus to talk about what it was like to organize and launch a fund. The result was the creation of the first version of a pitch deck for what would become Hillside Ventures, named for the road that carries the address of the business school. Next, the group built out what the areas of investment would be, and then they targeted raising $1 million for the first fund.

The approach to fundraising was innovative. Rather than seeking one or two large donors, they created three donor levels—$25,000, $50,000, and $75,000—to be given over three years. The idea was also to engage those donors in advisory roles. In less than a month, just prior to the campus shutting down due to COVID-19, Hillside had commitments for the full $1 million, dubbed the Genesis Fund.

"When it's real, when money is on the line, the energy goes way up," explains Greg Reilly, who oversees Hillside. "You can take a course that says, 'We're going to do case studies on X,' or you can join Hillside where we are really going to do X. It's just night-and-day energy. And the world reacts very differently to engagement than it does to case studies."

The program is structured into three sections, with students progressing through different roles over three semesters. New students focus on learning, the middle cohort does the primary work, and the most experienced students serve as leaders. Throughout their time in the program, students contribute to the Hillside website and podcast discussing venture capital investing.

Hillside seeks to invest in early-stage investments, which are pre-seed to Series A investments. (Series A is an investment in a private startup that has shown the potential to grow and generate revenue.) The fund originally focused on three verticals: **Education Technology (EdTech)**, **Insurance Technology (InsurTech)**, and **Sustainability**—and then added a fourth, **Sports Technology (SportsTech)**. However, if there is a UConn alumnus among a startup's management team, Hillside can invest regardless of the industry. If there is no UConn connection, Hillside will limit its investments in startups within the four verticals. Investments are up to $25,000 (though in rare cases can be increased to $50,000) with the opportunity for follow-on funding as the company grows.

EdTech is the relatively new field of study that integrates technology into the teaching and learning process. It is now used by primary and secondary schools, corporations, governments, and NGOs. Worldwide EdTech spending has jumped dramatically, from $183 billion in 2019 to a projected $404 billion in 2025, according to UConn School of Business statistics. It consists of the building blocks upon which the future of learning, development, and growth in the world will be built in the twenty-first century. The three main concepts are technology tools, teaching strategies, and the learning environment.

InsurTech was a natural choice for Hillside, given that nearby Hartford has been dubbed "the insurance capital of the world."

The insurance business has evolved dramatically with the introduction of new technologies that have both improved efficiency and increased customer service. The functions of an InsurTech startup can include pricing, underwriting, billing, and claims. Many companies are now involved in nontraditional areas such as pet coverage, and insurance for gig workers and cyberattacks.

Sustainability was an obvious choice because UConn is on the leading edge of sustainability among our nation's universities. Hillside defines sustainability startups as "companies that address environmental, social, and economic crises by providing sustainable solutions and/or mitigating factors that inhibit sustainability." A large part of this vertical is focused on climate change, as climate technology and alternative energy startups are a large and rapidly growing field.

SportsTech was also a rather obvious choice, given that UConn has won eleven NCAA women's basketball championships and six for the men. This burgeoning field covers everything from name, image, and likeness (NIL) to startups that focus on fan engagement, player health, and performance enhancement. Recently enacted by the NCAA, NIL allows college athletes to seek endorsements and be directly compensated while in school.

My donation supported adding a STEM (science, technology, engineering, and mathematics) fund as a fifth vertical in the fall of 2022. This vertical is unique in that it is a separate class from the Genesis Fund covering the other four verticals. STEM is also composed of mostly students outside the business school and a separate investment board from the other four verticals. I like that STEM draws from across the university and gives students in different disciplines a chance to explore their entrepreneurial ideas. In the spring semester of 2024, there was even a music major and a physics major in the class.

Each vertical is composed of a team of students. They begin by sourcing deals themselves and conducting a review of the possible investments with the support of advisors. Their due diligence on a particular startup is distributed to the six-person investment board for further analysis and research.

The students present two different deliverables. The first is a one-pager presented to the investment board, summarizing what is known about the company so far, what its highlights are, what the competition is, and what other risks come with potential investment. If the board reacts favorably to the one-pager, its members provide feedback so that the students can return to the startup and dig deeper. The student team then writes a ten- to fifteen-page investment deck and presents it to the board. If the board approves, the investment is made, and that startup becomes part of Hillside's portfolio.

"We get the chance to present ideas to the board, see the types of questions they ask, and also understand when to look into certain things further," explains Dhanush Kotumraju, a finance major in the class of 2024. "That type of experience at the undergraduate level prepares you for the workforce. You learn to take criticism and not to take things personally, and you learn to look at the bigger picture. Learning that at this stage makes us better prepared for our careers and for investment board presentations if we go into investing roles."

The investment process is nothing if not rigorous. Consider that in the fall semester of 2023, for instance, the sustainability vertical examined and rejected ninety potential deals at one stage or another.

By early 2024, the Hillside portfolio was doing well on paper, given the early stages of its investments. Four companies were valued at a multiple of what Hillside had invested, and only one, an educational gaming company, had been written down to zero. Those firms that were succeeding were looking for additional capital to grow even further.

EnviCore, which creates sustainable solutions for mining and construction industries, was valued at 1.5 times Hillside's investment, as was Natrion, a solid-state battery maker seeking to reduce the use of flammable liquids in large batteries. Infraclear, an AI company that gathers and scales multiple points of infrastructure data, had increased by 1.6x, and Otonomi, an insurance platform that provides underwriting, claims automation, and digital funds management services, had doubled in value. Life Legacy, a software company that creates wills and trusts, was exploring selling to a competitor, which could make that firm the first deal to cash out.

One of Hillside's most notable successes came through the efforts of Joseph Roberts, who found **Voltpost** at an entrepreneurship conference in Boston. As mentioned in the previous chapter, Voltpost is an electric vehicle charging platform that retrofits lampposts into high-speed charging stations that have twenty feet of retractable cable and can accommodate two to four charging ports.

As the students were putting together a presentation for a Hillside investment in Voltpost, it was fortuitous timing that David Samuels was on campus as a guest speaker to the Hillside Ventures class, describing his role as an advisor, investor, and board member in SemaConnect, a market-leading electric vehicle charging company. SemaConnect had been scaled with a national rollout, recapitalized with a top-tier private equity sponsor, and positioned for exit during the frothy market period in 2022. The company was acquired by a publicly traded suitor to create one of the largest EV charging networks in the United States.

David, a UConn alum and six-time CFO at publicly traded and private equity-sponsored technology companies, had considerable experience in and knowledge of the EV space. He agreed to come aboard as an adviser to Hillside. Here's what David says:

> Joseph presented the opportunity of this company in the EV charging space that was trying to solve a problem for how you get connectivity to EVs sitting in a city street/urban location without having a cable laid across the sidewalk. He'd done a lot of homework. I introduced him to a number of people in the marketplace so he could get some intel on the EV space. I did talk to the company as well, which he had asked me to do as sort of a key opinion leader in this case, and I got some intel from the company that I shared with Joseph that enabled his team to make a sound business decision.

There was some negotiating to be done. Voltpost was looking for investors that could put in a minimum of $100,000, but Hillside's stated maximum was $25,000 per company. Voltpost eventually agreed to lower the amount to $50,000, and the Hillside board agreed to step up.

Since the Hillside investment, Voltpost has executed on its promise. It has expanded operations from New York to Chicago, San Francisco, and Detroit, and it closed a further $3.6 million round of seed funding in July 2023. The company's goal is to move into more urban areas with its charging stations, which offer a lower-cost alternative to digging up the streets to install charging stations.

While financial returns are important, the true measure of Hillside's success lies in its educational impact. David Samuels emphasizes the learning opportunities these experiences provide: "The value of Hillside is understanding how to use critical thinking skills to evaluate an investment," he says, "and what the most important aspects are of a company you are considering investing in. It's great to challenge the students to understand new markets and new ways of doing things, to think through the applications of this technology or idea in the real world."

David teaches students to ask fundamental questions: What's the value proposition of the product or service? What problem is being solved? What's the total addressable market and competitive set? Are there regulatory issues to deal with? Is the business scalable, and does it have a capable management team? David goes on to say the following:

> When I ask students, "What is the single most important factor to evaluate as you consider an investment in a company?" some say it's the total addressable market (market size). Others say it's the quality of the product, or it's the intellectual property, or it's the price points. And I say, "No, it's management, management, management. That is what is going to make or break any investment decision." By going through the investment process at Hillside, students are seeing how good managers run these startups—because they get to talk to the founders. This also causes them to think about how they would run the business.

David has also emphasized a counterpoint to more conventional startup investment thinking. He tells students to look for companies that are "red ocean," a term for companies in an existing market with many competitors, as opposed to "blue ocean," which are companies entering a market yet to be discovered.

"These are companies that have a really good product that a larger player might want to buy to consolidate a growing market," he explains. "This allows you to maximize your investment quicker. I would put Voltpost in that category."

The success of these programs has also helped attract more alumni involvement. Rich Eldh, a successful entrepreneur who cofounded the business-to-business startup SiriusDecisions that was sold to Forrester Research for $245 million, explains: "Any financial return will be gravy. The mere fact that students can go through the process of real-world sourcing and research and then actually invest money and examine their thoughts and their due diligence, that's the real key."

The impact of Hillside Ventures extends far beyond individual investments and returns. In January 2024, Hillside expanded its reach with the launch of Hillside Private Capital. As mentioned in the previous chapter, Hillside Private Capital is a collaboration with Fortress Investment Group that allows students to shadow investment professionals working on actual deals, and it made UConn the first university to partner with a major Wall Street private equity firm in this way.

In the program, assignments are created against an analysis of the decks on current and prospective investments that Fortress sends to the students; then students run the numbers and do the analysis as best they can. The Fortress deal team leaders get together with the students, who pepper them with questions about why they did what they did. They also offer feedback on the students' analysis of the deals. This experience allows students to hone financial modeling skills to conduct due diligence on a product's offerings.

The success of Hillside has also helped build support for more funding from the state legislature. "If you can build that entrepreneurial spirit that drives new innovation, that's a great asset to the state," Rich Eldh says. "Entrepreneurship is one of those things that it's hard not to agree with, no matter where you are in your political beliefs—because regarding growth and innovation, I don't know anyone in the US that doesn't believe in that or want to support it."

Looking to the future, Hillside plans to expand its reach and impact. The program is exploring new verticals, including healthcare technology and artificial intelligence. There are also plans to increase the size of the fund and to create more opportunities for students from diverse backgrounds to participate.

The students themselves have become ambassadors for the program. "I tell every new freshman coming into the school of business that there's no better time to be at UConn because there are so many opportunities to get your foot in the door and get real-world experience to help you, whether you go into a career in finance or start your own venture," says Joseph Roberts. "It feels like we've created an incubator for individuals who want to get their ideas off the ground or help others do that."

Through programs like Hillside Ventures, that vision is becoming a reality, one student and one investment at a time. The program stands as a testament to what people can achieve when academic institutions embrace innovation, take calculated risks, and invest in their students' future. It's exactly the kind of program that Bud Boucher, with his entrepreneurial spirit and belief in the power of learning by doing, would have appreciated and supported. His legacy lives on in each student who learns to evaluate opportunities, manage risk, and bring innovative ideas to market—skills that took him decades to acquire through trial and error, but that these students are learning in a structured, supportive environment.

Perhaps most importantly, Hillside Ventures represents a new model for entrepreneurship education—one that combines rigorous academic study with real-world experience, that brings together students from different disciplines, and that emphasizes both the business and human aspects of entrepreneurship.

EPILOGUE: THE UCONN HUSKY EFFECT

THE ELEVEN NCAA NATIONAL CHAMPIONSHIPS that the women's team has won—including ten since 2000 with six perfect seasons—and the six titles the men have captured, with five since 2011, have helped the university build a national brand, created tremendous pride within the student body, and even brought notice to professors attending academic conferences. The basketball dynasty has also dramatically increased the number and the quality of applicants. This is part of the banner headline for the Husky Effect, creating a feeling of excellence that filters down through the entire university.

After the men's team won their fifth NCAA championship in 2023, applications for the 2024 fall semester hit a record high with more than 56,700 applicants and rose to more than 60,000 in the fall of 2025. This was an increase from the previous records of 48,000 in 2023 and 43,000 in 2022. The school of business also saw a 15 percent rise in 2025. Of course, there are other contributing factors, notably the university's rise in the various academic national rankings.

Sustaining this excellence requires the financial backing of the alumni, which numbers more than 282,000 worldwide. As you may recall from an earlier chapter, since the inception of name, image, and likeness (NIL) in 2021, two alumni-driven NIL collectives, Bleeding Blue for Good and the D'Amelio Huskies Collective, have been established to support student athletes while encouraging community engagement.

But while sports may have been a pillar of building UConn's network, other organizations have recently stepped up to broaden support and get the word out about the strong academic programs, the achievements of UConn graduates, and how vital the university is to the state of Connecticut. UConn Strong was created in 2017 to take the lead in advancing and serving its community of supporters by talking about the impact of UConn on the state's economy and culture.

"The network is critically important to the futures of the graduates," explains Rich Eldh, a member of the UConn Foundation board of directors. "At the University of Connecticut, this is a work in progress. When you look at the achievements UConn grads have made, there's a lot of very, very successful people. If we can put a focus on them and involve them, the network will become a critical part of UConn's success, just as it has for other universities."

Already, this expanded network is yielding results. The university can point to successful graduates like Dean Mahoney, who built 'Merican Mule into a regional beverage company; Emily Yale, whose Land Maverick is revolutionizing chemical applications on golf courses, and Hayley Segar, whose women's swimwear company, onewith, grew from her apartment into a successful online business. In early 2025, Segar appeared on *Shark Tank*, the competitive entrepreneurship TV show with almost three million viewers.

The entrepreneurial programs are also attracting former residents and alumni back to Connecticut to launch businesses. As Rich Eldh notes, "People know about Silicon Valley; they know about Stanford; they know about Berkeley, and all of the things that those schools have brought to the Valley. I think you might see that being replicated here in Connecticut."

The ultimate goal is to build UConn's network around excellence in all areas, nurtured by everyone who is a part of it, and do things for the greater good that benefit society as a whole. Just as UConn's basketball success has helped attract better student athletes, its rising academic reputation is drawing stronger applicants across all fields. The average GPA and test scores of admitted students continue to rise, while the university maintains its commitment to accessibility and diversity. This combination of excellence and opportunity is creating a powerful engine for economic and social mobility.

Toni and Bud Boucher

When I think about Bud's entrepreneurial journey—the successes and failures, the persistence and creativity—I see in these new programs the support system he never had. Each student who learns to evaluate risk properly, who understands the importance of finding the right partners, who gains hands-on experience in bringing ideas to market, represents a dream realized not just for themselves but for all the entrepreneurs who came before them.

The transformation of UConn has become about the very qualities that define successful entrepreneurs. The Boucher Management & Entrepreneurship Department and programs like Hillside Ventures are helping to ensure that future entrepreneurs have the support, knowledge, and experience they need to make their journeys successful ones.

President Radenka Maric's vision for UConn's future encompasses this holistic approach to education and success. "When people ask what UConn is known for, most people around the state or the country now say basketball," she says. "But I tell people that what I want in ten years when you ask that question is for people to say that UConn is known as a national and global leader in taking on and solving the pressing issues that humanity has faced and continues to face. That is the Husky Nation we all want to belong to."

The Husky Nation we're building isn't just about sports victories or academic achievements—it's about creating a community that nurtures innovation, encourages risk-taking, and supports those who dare to dream big. It's about maintaining Connecticut's legacy as a cradle of American innovation while preparing for the challenges of tomorrow.

In the end, that's the greatest legacy we can leave—not just teaching students how to succeed in business but helping them understand how their success can contribute to something larger than themselves. That's the spirit of entrepreneurship at its finest, and that's the future we're building at UConn.

PHOTO CREDITS

Courtesy of the University of Connecticut: pgs. 6, 14, 71, 77, 78.

Courtesy of Toni Boucher: pgs. 25, 26, 36, 57, 69, 101.

Courtesy of Aria Penna: pg. 83.

The insitutitional mark on page 109 used by permission of the University of Connecticut.

ABOUT THE AUTHOR

TONI BOUCHER is serving her first four-year term as Wilton's First Selectman (mayor) after a lengthy career in public service for the state of Connecticut and the town of Wilton. She is also serving on some of the nation's top hospital and foundation boards. Her positions have included board of education chairman, selectman, state board of education commissioner, state vo-tech board of education member, advisory board member of the Connecticut Office of the Child Advocate, state representative minority leader, and state senate chief deputy minority leader.

Boucher has run in seventeen political campaigns (and won fifteen). She and her late husband, Bud, have been involved in many startups and business innovations. Each of these involved risk and belief in pursuit of an idea even when others lose faith. Bud, along with Toni Boucher's father, who brought the family to the United States when she was a little girl, have inspired her over a lifetime. Despite countless business failures, they never gave up until they found success.

Boucher's career in the private sector includes executive leadership roles in large businesses where she developed billion-dollar budgets and led new business development and marketing initiatives. She recently retired as a director of a leading $30 billion asset management company. Boucher has founded several startups and is now helping the University of Connecticut Business School grow its entrepreneurship and student-run investment programs.

She has held Series 7, 63, and 31 brokerage licenses and has an MBA from UConn. Boucher also published a white paper on "Ethics and the Nonprofit." Sitting on numerous nonprofit boards that fund new programs and research, she is a forty-year resident of Wilton and has three children and six grandchildren.

As Wilton's Chief Executive Officer and Chief Administrative Officer, Boucher's full-time responsibilities include day-to-day administration of the town, its infrastructure, economic development, and town security, as well as collaborating with the board of selectmen.

toni.boucher.18
toni-boucher

JOSH YOUNG has written five *New York Times* bestsellers, four additional *Los Angeles Times* bestsellers, and five books made into feature documentaries with and about leading experts in the worlds of business, law, entertainment, science, comedy, natural history, exploration, sports, fashion, and politics.

FOR MORE INFORMATION, PLEASE VISIT
JOSHYOUNGAUTHOR.COM.

UCONN
UNIVERSITY OF CONNECTICUT

See how the UConn School of Business is shaping the entrepreneurs of the future.

**DISCOVER
THE HUSKY EFFECT
YOURSELF.**

www.business.uconn.edu

www.ingramcontent.com/pod-product-compliance
Lightning Source LLC
LaVergne TN
LVHW051034070526
838201LV00009B/194